# Study Guide

Your Journey into Habitation with the Living God

## MARIE FOWLER

LIVING STONES STUDY GUIDE

Copyright © 2020 by Marie Fowler

All rights reserved.

No part of this manuscript may be used or reproduced in any matter whatsoever without written permission from the publisher, except in the case of brief quotations embodied in critical articles and reviews.

FIRST EDITION

Maon Publishing

ISBN-10:978-0-578-64509-4

ISBN-13:978-0-578-64509-4

This companion Study derives its context and quotes from *Living Stones.* Marie Fowler, Lake Wales, FL: Maon Media, 2017.

Unless otherwise marked, Scripture quotations are taken from the NEW AMERICAN STANDARD BIBLE®, Copyright © 1960, 1962, 1963, 1968, 1971, 1972, 1973, 1975, 1977, 1995 by The Lockman Foundation. Used by permission.

Scripture quotations marked "KJV" are taken from the Holy Bible, King James Version (Public Domain).

Front Cover: "New Jerusalem" by Spencer Williams/ www.jesuspaintings.com used by artist permission, additional cover design and interior format by Marie Fowler. Author photograph by Jennifer Miskov. Editor Jennifer Westbrook. Maon Media logo by Francisco Rodriguez Guerrero of Esh Graphic Design.

All images and graphics used by permission or under paid license with Canva at www.canva.com and www.pngtree.com

Author website: www.allgloriouswithin.com

# Study Guide

Your Journey into Habitation with the Living God

## MARIE FOWLER

# Dedication

This study guide is lovingly dedicated to my Abba Father.
In my quest to know You I found myself.


And also . . .


To the mystical lovesick Bride who is unsatisfied with status quo:


Keep diving deeper into the mysteries of Abba's heart. The real adventure begins when you long to know Him as He wants to be known.

# Also by Marie Fowler

LIVING STONES: Your Journey into Habitation with the Living God

: The Greatest Love Story Ever Told, Volume I

# Table of Contents

Note from the Author     9

Introduction     11

1. Your Journey into Habitation     21

2. Reuben: The Passionate Lover     25

3. Simeon: The Zealous Hearer     40

4. Levi: The Priestly Bride     51

5. Judah: The Government of Praise     65

6. Dan: The Voice of Justice     83

7. Naphtali: The Doe Set Free!     96

8. Gad: Habitation of God's Fortune     107

9. Asher: The Spring of Joy!     119

# Table of Contents

10. Issachar: The Humble Burden Bearer — 136

11. Zebulun: The Haven for Souls — 151

12. Manasseh: The Forgiving One — 164

13. Ephraim: The Fruitful Vine — 179

14. Benjamin: The Beloved — 190

15. The New Jerusalem: Your Journey into Habitation — 205

*Living Stones* Study Guide Answer Key — 217

Bibliography — 234

Resources — 235

About the Author — 238

## A Note from the Author...

The journey you are about to embark on with the Father will forever mark you. You see, Beloved, destiny has placed *Living Stones* and this companion Study Guide across your path at this divinely appointed time. It is no small thing. In fact, you are a very fulfillment of Scripture! In Genesis 49:1 Jacob prophesies to his twelve sons,

> "And Jacob called unto his sons, and said, *Gather yourselves together, that I may tell you that which shall befall you in the last days*"

In the faith chapter Hebrews 11:8–11 Abraham's covenant promise and long-time dream is seen,

> *"By faith Abraham, when he was called, obeyed by going out to a place which he was to receive for an inheritance; and he went out, not knowing where he was going. By faith he lived as an alien in the land of promise, as in a foreign land, dwelling in tents with Isaac and Jacob, fellow heirs of the same promise; for he was looking for the city which has foundations, whose architect and builder is God."*

And ultimately the Kingdom mandate of Christ himself as it reads in Isaiah 49:6,

> *"It is too small a thing that You should be My Servant,* **To raise up the tribes of Jacob**"

The culmination of the Father's dream is revealed in us, His sons and daughters—Abba's dream is a holy habitation built of Living Stones (I Peter 2:4–6, Romans 8:19, Ephesians 2:19–22). This is His big dream of family fulfilled! Without you Abba's house and dream would be incomplete. Time is hastening to its glorious climax, and many like you are being "revealed," ushering in the new *Kingdom Glorious* reign of Messiah. It is time to take a deep look into the mirror of God's Word. Only the Spirit can truly reveal your true identity (tribe) hidden in Christ. For such a time as this, *Living Stones* is your hand to discover the "*the mystery which has been hidden from the past ages and generations, but has now been manifested in His saints . . . Christ within you, the* **hope of Glory**." The tribes

## A Note from the Author

contain important insight into the spiritual identity of the *"new self which is being renewed to a true knowledge of the One who created him, a renewal in which there is no Jew nor Greek."*

Finding your tribe is a true supernatural adventure that will bring radical transformation. It is paramount to know that you will get as much out of this journey as you put into it, meaning you must be diligent to do the heart work. Be like the Bereans and seek out Scripture for yourself. This Study Guide is designed to ask heart-provoking questions more than theological knowledge (though it certainly contains solid biblical theology). If your quest is to know Him, you in turn will not only find Him but yourself—for you are a mirror of Him!
The activation exercises are meant to equip you within your gifts and callings. Perhaps you may even discover hidden gifts and spiritual DNA traits you never knew you possessed. Journal activities are an intimate time of fellowship and discovery where you find the treasure within you.

Many have asked me is it possible to be more than one tribe. My thoughts are no, you do have dominant spiritual DNA markers: this is your tribe. Your tribe is your unique spiritual makeup that mirrors facets of the Father you were designed to embody and display. Abba's children do not have split personalities. This being said, it is easy to identify with other tribes' traits. I advise people to understand how other tribes' traits mirror your tribe and to learn what other tribes have to teach you. For example, as a Levite I can learn mercy (which is not a "natural inclination" for Levi) from brothers in the tribe of Manasseh. We are all in Abba's classroom and can equally glean and learn from one another. The tribes are a beautiful example of this. Maximize your transformation and gain insight from your own tribe as well as the rest of the family of God (other tribes). We each possess keys of destiny for each other. It is a way to bear one another's burdens by first learning to "walk a mile in their shoes"!

Note this Study Guide is a tool of transformation. It is ideal for both personal devotions as well as group study. At no time should there be any form of grading of answers. An answer key is included in the back of this book, but only as a guide. The true test or grade comes from the transformation that occurs within you. Only the Holy Spirit can test and prove the work done within our hearts. To truly immerse yourself in this revelation, take your time, do not hurry out of the revelation given. Marinate on each rich insight given and then dig even deeper. Accompany your study times with deep times of contemplative prayer, worship, and journaling. This will ensure that you will receive the most out of the experience provided by this Study. There are optional creative exercises to heighten and challenge your growth. Acceleration comes to the hungry and diligent. When you seek Him with your whole heart, His Word promises you will find Him. Dive deep into this ancient mystery—for destiny awaits!

In His radiant love and shalom,

*Marie Fowler*

# Introduction

1. How would you define worth?

2. How do you see the Father?

3. How does the Father see you? (Be honest and give an answer not from head knowledge of what you think you "should say," but rather how you truly feel.)

4. How have you engaged in self-doubt as a son or daughter of God (past or present)?

Introduction

5. What is the Hebrew word for habitation? _____

6. Describe how you would interpret the meaning of habitation in your walk with the Lord.

7. How has the finished work of the Cross afforded us habitation?

8. Creation is longing for the revealing of the sons and daughters of God. How has the identity crisis (the orphan spirit) affected mankind?

How have you struggled with your own identity? What lies do you believe right now about yourself? Ask Father God five things about your identity in Christ.

- ❖ **Optional Creative Activity**: What is Abba's dream for you? Create a dream board from what He speaks to you. (You can use photos from magazines or graphics online, found objects that hold significant meaning, song lyrics, etc. Have fun!)

9. Research the word *identity* in Hebrew. Abba's dream for His sons and daughters began before the earth was formed. Study and meditate on Ephesians 1:3–12. Journal how the Holy Spirit speaks to you through this.

10. What are you looking to receive on this journey of discovering your identity in Christ?

11. List some misconceptions a religious mindset has made of the Father.

12. List some misconceptions the world has of God.

13. What are your own misconceptions of the Father?

14. What is the common thread between your answers in questions 10–12?

15. The tribes teach us not only to know who we truly are, but to know our brothers and sisters by the Spirit and not the flesh (**II Corinthians 5:16**). In the exercise below, list how knowing your brothers and sisters (and yourself) by the flesh and then by knowing one another by the Spirit manifests.

| **FLESH** | **SPIRIT** |
|---|---|
|   |   |

16. How have you misjudged yourself and others by the flesh?

Introduction

# ACTIVATION EXERCISE

Ask Holy Spirit some creative ways to see yourself and others by the Spirit and list them below. Then ask Holy Spirit for a strategy to begin to implement this in your everyday life.

17. The tribes reveal _____ we are in Abba's image and our _____ He designed.

18. Study Ephesians Chapter 2. Take time and feast on it, one section at a time. Feel free to journal in addition to answering the questions below and do a deeper word study. This scripture is rich and foundational to the message about the tribes. Take your time and search out this meaty revelation.

    A. Verses 1–3 speak of who we were before we came to know Christ. In light of walking in the Spirit or in the flesh—as a child of God, does this pertain to you now?

    B. Contemplate the vastness of God's grace (verses 4–9). As an heir, seated with Christ in heavenly places, how is our sonship and place of dominion fueled by grace? What is your testimony of God's grace?

    C. The gifts (*charismata*) are known as spiritual graces (*charis,* Greek for *grace*). Our spiritual graces uniquely designed by God are given to us to join Him in what He is doing. What spiritual graces do you most prominently possess?

D. What facets of your unique spiritual graces mirror the Father's nature?

E. With this in mind, how can you relate this to intimacy with Him? How do you apply this in your everyday walk?

F. Read and reflect on verses 11–19. The Jewish people are called to be a light to the nations (Isaiah 49:6 and Acts 13:47). Scripture says, "Salvation is of the Jews" (John 4:22 and Romans 11), meaning God's heart was to first save His people, consecrate them unto Himself, and provide salvation for all mankind through the Jewish people (Yeshua). Yet today there is a false doctrine commonly believed that the Church (Gentile believers) has replaced Israel (known as Replacement Theology). How have you seen this operate in the Church today?

G. Have you yourself believed this because this is all you were taught?

H. How has this brought pain to the Jewish people?

I. How has Replacement Theology affected history?

## Introduction

19. Take time to study Ezekiel 37 and meditate on it. The end-time move of God (known as the One New Man movement) will be comprised of a company of sons and daughters who have awakened to the glory of God, taking place in Abba's *maon kadosh*, the tribes of Israel. How can we corporately pursue the restoration of the House of Israel? How can you personally pursue the restoration of Jew and Gentile?

20. What keys of destiny do the Jewish people hold for Gentiles?

21. What keys of destiny do Gentiles hold for the Jewish people?

22. In light of Abba's heart to restore the whole house of Israel (Jew and Gentile), ask the Holy Spirit for creative ways to implement change that promotes healing, understanding, and brings both as One New Man in Messiah into their destinies. How can you be intentional in relationship, ministry, and governmentally?

23. What are three ways God paints us a picture of His habitation in Scripture?

24. What are the four living creatures?

25. What are the four captain tribes, and what symbols were on their banners when they went out to war?

    1. Tribe-               Symbol-

    2. Tribe-               Symbol-

    3. Tribe-               Symbol-

    4. Tribe-               Symbol-

Now mediating on these four captain tribe symbols, how do you see Yeshua as each one?

**Optional Creative Activity:** In an intimate time of worship, paint one or all four of these captain tribes' typologies of Christ and how He is bringing you BREAKTHROUGH in your own life right now. Note: You may want to do them separately, together, or just the one that stands out to you the most. Poetry, music, or composing a worship dance piece are also options you may want to use.

# Chapter 1
## Your Journey into Habitation with the Living God

1. What does the Hebrew word *aliyah* mean?

2. Describe times you've walked in your God-given authority and when you haven't. What's the difference?

3. What is one of the biggest strongholds in most believers today?

4. How has the orphan spirit held you prisoner?

5. Our spiritual gifts are often referred to as spiritual "_____."

6. How has rejection hindered you from being who you truly are?

7. Study Deuteronomy 7:6. What does it mean to be God's own possession?

# Journal Activity

The Israelites lived in fear and dread of their enemies, when in fact their enemies were shaking in their boots, having heard of how God miraculously delivered the Israelites out of Egypt and destroyed their enemies. How has fear kept you wandering in the wilderness? List five declarations about leaving the wilderness and possessing your inheritance.

- ❖ **Optional Creative Activity**: Look online (For instance, YouTube, iTunes, or Spotify) for Don Potter's song "Take the Land" from the Morningstar album named *Vision*. During worship play this song. Visualize beforehand the giants that are hindering you from your Promised Land. Find a creative way to knock down those giants using found objects. Then symbolically reenact crossing the Jordan River into your inheritance as you make your five declarations. **\*Hint:** *You may very well get more than five declarations!*

8. Meditating on Romans 8:19, how could the "revealing of the sons and daughters of God" manifest the end-time move of God in light of Habakkuk 2:14?

9. We are no longer _____, so we need to live like we are _____ because _____ coupled with _____ is how we can live in _____ reality!

10. What is a façade?

11. How have you entertained striving to be like God (facades) versus knowing who you truly are in His image? What conflicts, trauma, disappointments, and deception rob you from intimacy?

## ACTIVATION EXERCISE

Stand in front of a full-length mirror. Take a depth breath, close your eyes, and ask the Holy Spirit eight lies you're believing about yourself right now. Now open your eyes and really look into the mirror intently and **RENOUNCE** the **EIGHT LIES** one by one. Now take a second-deep breath, close your eyes, and ask the Holy Spirit for **EIGHT TRUTHS** to **DECLARE**. Open your eyes, looking deeply into the mirror once more, declare the eight truths the Holy Spirit gave you. Note: It may be a good idea to journal this and/or process this with someone you trust, perhaps even do the exercise together. Remember this activity when you come to your tribe's chapter in this Study Guide. It will most likely be in some ways mirroring the strengths and the facades found within your tribe. It is also a good idea to revisit this activity when covering the facades and strengths of your tribe, dialoging deeper with the Holy Spirit as you pursue freedom and discovering your identity.

**Activation Exercise continued…**

To help you get started, it would also be profitable to review the strengths and facades indicated in your *Spiritual DNA Test* results (You may take the test at our website: www.allgloriouswithin.com/spiritualdnatest)

12. The spirit of _____ will keep us out of _____ as the Bride of Christ, but more importantly, it will keep us from our Father's greatest desire of _____ with Him and living in _____ reality.

13. How has this spirit hindered you in your spiritual family? How have you partnered with this spirit against someone else within spiritual family?

14. What cannot live where a lie remains?

# Chapter 2

## Reuben: The Passionate Lover

1. Meditate on I Corinthians 13:1–7. Do a word study on the word *love* in Hebrew and Greek. Note the differences between the different types of the word *love*.

**Hebrew:**

**Greek:**

2. Genesis 29 speaks of the circumstances of Reuben's birth. How could this form his identity?

3. How do you see yourself in Reuben's story?

4. What does the name of Reuben mean?

5. What does love to do?

6. What is the Hebrew root word for *ben*, and what does it mean?

Meditating on the Hebrew word in the previous question above, how can you build the Father's house as his son or daughter? What does this look like both internally for you and corporately as part of God's family? What value does the Father say you add to building His holy habitation with Him? How can you, as a vital member of God's family, develop a healthy, thriving community now?

**Optional Creative Activity**: Host and organize a "Love Feast." Invite members of your faith family and edify one another by calling out the gold (the glory of God—true identity, strengths, gifts) in and how grateful you are for each other over a meal and fellowship time. Take time to listen to each other's dreams and promises God has given individually, and then pray over one another concerning this.

7. What is the gemstone of Reuben, and what does it symbolize?

8. Meditating on the depth of the meaning of Yeshua's shed blood, what wealth has God's love and forgiveness by His blood brought you?

9. What is your testimony of being truly forgiven and redeemed? What are you grateful for?

10. Make five declarations concerning redemption through Yeshua's blood, forgiveness, and God's love concerning your identity.

11. Do a Hebrew word study on the word *blood,* and then meditate upon it.

12. What are the symbols of Reuben?

13. Meditate and study the following scriptures within the context of the book and then answer the questions below them: Judges 5:31, Psalm 50:1–2, Psalm 110:1–3, Hosea 6:2–3, II Samuel 23:3–4, Psalm 57:8, Zephaniah 3:5, Isaiah 58:8, and Malachi 4:2a.

    A. Who is "the rising sun"?

    B. The rising sun speaks of the _____ and message of _____ within the spiritual DNA of every _____.

    C. What are Reubenites carriers of?

## Journal Activity

Meditating on the meaning of the rising sun, how has Yeshua brought you a new day? If you are struggling with disappointment, ask the Lord for three declarations of hope for your new day. Make these three declarations of hope for one week every day while intentionally engaging in a negativity fast (speech and thought life). Speak only in the affirming, positive light of how the Father sees you and what He is doing in your life. Journal about this experience.

14. What does the symbol of the mandrake plant mean?

15. Reuben is a _____.

16. Read and meditate on Genesis 30:14–17. How could Reuben's gift to Leah have affected her? How do you feel this displays the love of God?

17. In your own words describe sacrificial love.

18. How is the Lord calling you to lay down your own life for Him . . . for others?

## Journal Activity

In a time of intimate worship, envision yourself under the apple tree with Yeshua. What is He speaking to you? Journal about your experience.

19. What are the three motivational gifts the tribe of Reuben possesses? If you are a Reubenite, how do these three motivational gifts manifest in your life?

## ACTIVATION EXERCISE

If you are a Reuben, ask the Holy Spirit how the Father wants to use you in these motivational gifts in a creative way to evangelize (i.e. helping the homeless, writing love letters or words of encouragement to random people the Holy Spirit highlights to you, or other random acts of kindness). Allow Reuben's story to inspire you. List them below and implement them under the Holy Spirit's guidance. You may even want to coordinate a small ministry team to carry out this activation.

## JACOB'S PROPHECY

**The following questions and journal activity coincide with Jacob's prophecy to the tribe of Reuben.**

17. Meditate and study Genesis 49: 3–4, Jacob's prophecy to Reuben, within the context of the book. Answer the questions below:

    A. What do you feel Jacob was really saying when he prophesied to Reuben: *"Reuben, you are my first-born; My might and the beginning of my strength."*

B. What could this mean for you personally if you are from the tribe of Reuben? If you are not from this tribe, how can you champion and affirm your brother and sister Reubenites?

C. What does living a life of excellence mean for a believer? How can we possess godly excellence and honor from a place of intimacy?

D. Where in your life have you exhibited behaviors of being "uncontrolled as water." What has conforming to the flesh cost you?

E. Ask the Father what lies you have believed to be uncontrolled as water. Then ask Him to give you a revelation of how to make you stable from a place in His love. Note: You might want to journal about this!

F. Have you personally struggled with the façade of lust? If yes, how has this caused you to lose sight of true intimacy and undermine your true value and identity?

20. For a Reubenite, to lose _____ of the _____ of love causes him to lose his spiritual _____, for love is his place of _____!

21. In your own words, describe the gift of sexual intimacy given to us by God and why it is so precious.

22. Why is accountability crucial in the area of sexual sin? How can we truly love without condemning our brothers and sisters who struggle with the façade of lust? How can we call the gold (the glory) out of them and not the dirt?

23. If you struggle with the façade of lust, pray this prayer:

Abba, I long to be free from the sin of lust. I repent of not valuing the gift of sexual intimacy. I repent for not valuing myself and how beautiful You truly made me. I renounce the spirit of lust in Yeshua's name! Yeshua, forgive me of walking away from intimacy with you. I've looked for intimacy outside of You. Only You can complete me. Forgive me for looking for what I thought was love in all the wrong places. Remove the scales of rejection from my eyes. Let me see who I am as your Bride . . . whole and complete. Help me to come to a place where I can truly say You are enough God, You are all I need, only You can satisfy me.

  Abba, I know You have a plan for my life, one where I can share true holy sexual intimacy with the mate You have for me or have already given me. I ask for you to heal where I have been wounded sexually. You are my worth. I am whole, worthy, needed, worth waiting for, and worth fighting for.
In Yeshua's name, Amen.

Reuben: The Passionate Lover

# ACTIVATION EXERCISE

As a token of dedicating yourself to the Lord for true purity and to value your worth, purchase a white rose or jewelry (i.e. a ring or necklace). Under the leading of the Holy Spirit, write your marriage vows to the Lord and His to you. Also write a letter to your spouse (current or future) of the value of purity and love you are committed to (present or future tense) to consecrate your lives as holy unto the Lord.

24. In Korah's rebellion there were a few from the tribe of Reuben who compromised by following him in revolt against Moses, and it cost them dearly. How has compromise cost you your place of intimacy, authority, and destiny? When have you partnered with the wrong company? How did you grow from the experience?

25. How has repentance led you back into your place of intimacy, authority, and destiny?

26. In Moses' prophecy he states, *"May Reuben live and not die, nor his men be few."* How can this manifest today in the Kingdom for the tribe of Reuben?

When Reuben, Gad, and half of Manasseh settled on the wrong side of the Jordan, they settled for less than Abba's best for them. How have you compromised your inheritance? What is the Father's desire for your inheritance?

27. God cannot truly entrust us with our _____ nature unless we relinquish our _____ nature.

28. Study and meditate on Genesis 37:18–22. Who do you feel Reuben represents and why? How do you display this representation and why?

29. The tribe of Reuben has an evangelistic gifting and heartbeat for souls. If you are from the tribe of Reuben, how does this manifest in your life? How do you feel called to the ministry of reconciliation? What is your motivation?

30. Reuben's captain tribal symbol is the man. How do you see Yeshua in this symbol? How do you (if you are from this tribe) identify this symbol?

31. Read Genesis 37:18–22. How do you see Yeshua in the character of Reuben—the selfless older brother?

32. In I Chronicles 26:31–32 we see the tribe of Reuben restored to their God-given identity and leadership. How does the Father want to restore you to your God-given identity and leadership?

33. How is the Father restoring your dominion through intimacy?

# 12 Declarations for the Tribe of Reuben

1. I am a WORTHY and a MUCH-LOVED son/daughter of God.

2. God's LOVE causes me to SEE and be SEEN.

3. I am like the rising sun; BREAKTHROUGH is in my spiritual DNA.

4. Condemnation, discouragement, and hopelessness are not my portion. God's mercies for me are NEW EVERY MORNING!

5. I will LIVE and not DIE, and DECLARE the works of the Lord!

6. I REFUSE to settle for less than I was created for!

7. I WILL POSSESS the FULLNESS of my inheritance in Christ!

8. God has given me His STRENGTH. I am a stable, powerful, and MIGHTY WARRIOR!

9. The Father is my source of HOPE. All His promises are YES and AMEN!

10. I am the Beloved Bride of Yeshua. Under His apple tree He awakens me to pure and passionate love.

11. I am a PASSIONATE and CONTAGIOUS lover of God and people.

12. I am a VALUABLE and NEEDED *Living Stone* (ruby) in God's Holy Habitation. I am a foundational stone in God's family.

# Chapter 3

## Simeon: The Zealous Hearer

1. What is the Sh'ma?

2. In what scripture does Yeshua recite the Sh'ma?

3. What revelation do you see in the Sh'ma, and how can it relate to us today as worshipers?

4. The sense of _____ was given to us to _____ God's voice and _____ Him.

5. What does the name of Simeon mean?

6. What was Leah longing for when she gave birth to Simeon? How did God answer her through Simeon's birth?

7. Hearing is a spiritual discipline, weapon, and a valuable tool for deep intimacy. How has the Lord developed the gift of hearing in your life? Where are you lacking the spiritual discipline of hearing?

8. What is a Simeonite's spirit like? Do you see these characteristics in yourself? How can God use these characteristics for His Kingdom? What is He calling you to surrender in these characteristics?

9. Study and meditate on Deuteronomy 15:12–17 and Luke 1:38. What are some characteristics of a bondservant? What is the Holy Spirit speaking to you about being His bondservant?

10. How have you engaged in disgruntled slave's mindset versus a bondservant's heart?

11. How have you struggled to hear God's voice?

12. Describe times it was easy to hear God's voice. What was the Father doing in your life at that time? What was your heart position? How did this bring you breakthrough?

13. How hard has it been for you to discipline your soul to be still? Ask Holy Spirit for at least three things that hinder you from becoming still and hearing the voice of God.

*Be Still and Know*–Part A: In your worship time with the Lord, engage in an intentional time of silence for at least ten minutes. No praying, Bible reading, drawing, music, or distraction of any form, just silence. Engage in worship with Him in silence to hear Him and know Him. Repeat this activity every day for one week.

Reflect and journal about your experience with the Lord in the Activation Exercise *Be Still and Know*–Part A. What did God reveal to you? How has this transformed you?

14. The gemstone of Simeon is the _____ or _____.

15. What does Simeon's gemstone reveal? What must a Simeon rely on the Holy Spirit for?

16. How do you feel heeding wisdom plays a crucial role in hearing God?

17. When have you not heeded wisdom and resulted to either impetuous, foolish behavior or rebellion? How did the Father bring you back into intimacy with Him?

18. Describe your journey in the school of the Holy Spirit.

19. The tribe of Simeon has three symbols. What are they?

20. What are Simeonites a carrier of?

21. If you are Simeonite, how has the Holy Spirit led you in ministry in the area of words of knowledge, healing, evangelism, revival, and the prophetic? What is the Father's vision for you to operate in these areas in the future?

22. How do you personally relate to the symbol of the earthen pitcher with the Father? What has been your journey of being on the "potter's wheel" What does it mean to be pliable in the potter's hands?

23. How have you embraced brokenness before the Lord?

24. Simeonites are fierce warriors. How has God called you to battle?

25. Describe times you have engaged in battle from a place of intimacy, surrender, and allowing yourself to be still—hearing the Father's voice and proceeding with wisdom.

26. Describe times you warred in your own flesh impetuously or in anger. What chaos and confusion ensued? What did it cost you and others? How did the Father redeem each situation?

## Journal Activity

Noting the difference of when you've engaged in battle led by the Spirit and when you've engaged in battle in your flesh, what is the Father's heart for you as His zealous warrior? How can you burn for Him and souls from a place of intimacy?

# ACTIVATION EXERCISE

Find some soaking music and still your soul before the Lord. Ask Him to take you into the War Room of Heaven. What battle plans does He have for you on the table? What is He entrusting you with in His Kingdom? Write your battle strategies down and start to implement them.

27. Read Genesis 34:1–31. How do you relate to Simeon and Levi in this story?

28. How do you think God's solution would have aided Dinah if Simeon and Levi had sought Him instead?

29. How has injustice molded your perspective? Is any of your perspective faulty, or has it been fully redeemed

30. How does allowing anger, jealously, offense, and critical spirits into our habitation with the Lord keep us from intimacy?

31. Read Numbers 25:1–16. How can you relate to Zimri?

32. How has rebellion opened the door to deception and witchcraft in your life? How has rebellion affected your God-given gift of intimacy-hearing?

33. How has rebellion, either that you engaged in or someone else's rebellion, brought trauma into your life? How does the Father want to bring redemption and healing?

34. How has jealousy detoured your destiny?

35. Ask Holy Spirit what event(s) birthed the root of jealously in your life, and list them. What spirit was truly at work in these events?

36. Do you sometimes feel as if you are not enough?

37. Ask the Father to reveal your true worth. How does He want to turn jealousy into zealous passion for Him and others?

38. Study Peter's life and ministry. How can you identify with him?

39. How do you feel the tribe of Judah is valuable to the tribe of Simeon? How have they been valuable to you personally?

## ACTIVATION EXERCISE

*Be Still and Know*–Part B: In your worship time with the Lord, engage in an intentional time of silence for at least thirty minutes (same rules apply as before). Preface this time of silence with seeking His heart for revival. How does He want to use you in revival? You can do this activity every day for a week (or longer if you like).

Then in your day-to-day life, when you are out and about in public, ask the Holy Spirit if He would highlight three people to give a word of knowledge to for healing, then follow through and pray for them. Journal from your experience.

# 12 Declarations For the Tribe of Simeon

1. I am a fiery, ZEALOUS Bride of Yeshua! I BURN only for Him!

2. I was designed by my Heavenly Father to intimately HEAR and KNOW Him.

3. God has given me the priceless gift of WISDOM. I receive His wisdom through INTIMACY.

4. I OBEY God's voice because I KNOW His voice intimately.

5. I choose to be a LOVESICK and SURRENDERED bondservant and not a disgruntled rebellious slave.

6. I am a TAMED but FIERCE stallion that carries God's word!

7. As I be STILL and KNOW that He is really God, everything in my life ALIGNS with Heaven.

8. I choose to war only with the SWORD of the SPIRIT and not the sword of the flesh.

9. I am a vessel of great HONOR. I am PLIABLE in the hands of the Master Potter.

10. I will INCLINE my ears as a DISCIPLE of Christ.

11. When I am connected to PRAISE (Judah), I am UNSTOPPABLE in Christ.

12. REVIVAL is my DNA! By His Spirit I will IGNITE the world on fire and bring radical transformation to nations!

# Chapter 4

# Levi: The Priestly Bride

1. Study and meditate on John 4:23–24. What was Yeshua truly saying in this scripture? What does it mean to worship the Father in Spirit and in truth? How does the Word define a true worshiper?

2. As His Bride, how has the Lord chastened you for true intimacy?

3. Study Genesis 29:34. What was Leah going through prior to Levi's birth?

4. What does the name Levi mean in Genesis 29:34?

5. What was God revealing to Leah through Levi's birth? How did Levi's birth shift her relationship with Jacob? What is Leah's new revelation of who God is to her through Levi's birth?

6. What is the deeper mystery found in Ephesians 5:22–32?

7. What is the Hebrew name for *priest*? What does it mean?

8. Study and meditate on John 17:1–6. Do a word study on the Hebrew word *echad*.

Engage in a time of deep worship with the Bridegroom. Ask Yeshua to take you into His chamber room to encounter Him, face to face and heart to heart. How is He revealing Himself as your Bridegroom? What does He want to reveal to you as His priestly Bride?

**Optional Creative Activity**: A ketubah is a marriage contract between the Bridegroom and the Bride. Design your own ketubah with Yeshua. For inspiration there are many beautiful examples online. Ketubahs are known to be beautiful works of art that beautifully depict the marriage vows and celebrate the union of a Jewish couple. Be creative—put your unique personality and intimate journey with the Lord into the design of your ketubah.

9. What is the primary calling and destiny of every Levite?

10. What does the Hebrew word *K'vod* mean?

11. _____ is not based on works, but rather is birthed from a _____ heart, being desperate and poor in spirit and _____ by fire.

12. What is Levi's gemstone?

13. What does this gemstone symbolize for the tribe of Levi?

14. How can you personally identify with the symbolism behind Levi's gemstone?

15. How does the Lord draw you into being a walking PDA (public display of affection)? How does this manifest in your everyday walk with Him?

16. What fruit is tied to Levi's gemstone and why?

17. The tribe of Levi is a first fruits company. How do Levites embody this?

18. Why was Levite not numbered? How do you see the rich meaning of this in your intimate walk with the Lord?

19. Describe your life as an intercessor. (If you are not from the tribe of Levi or an intercessor, describe an intercessor's walk with the Lord whom you know personally. How has their life and intercession impacted you?) What motivates you as an intercessor? How can you grow as an intercessor?

20. In Hebraic thought the outer court is also known as the _____, the inner court is known as the _____, and the Holy of Holies is known as the _____.

21. Who in Scripture said He was all three—the inner court, outer court, and the Holy of Holies?

22. As a Levite, how do you identify with the brazen altar?

23. What does a life of sacrifice truly mean if born of intimacy? How have you embraced brokenness?

Levi: The Priestly Bride

24. What is the bronze laver a type and shadow of?

25. According to Jewish commentaries the bronze laver consisted of _____ _____?

26. What does the table of shewbread represent for the tribe of Levi?

27. How many loaves of bread were upon the table of shewbread? What do you feel this means prophetically?

28. What tribe made the bread, and why is it prophetic to their tribe?

# ACTIVATION EXERCISE

In a time of contemplative prayer ask the Father for a fresh revelation (fresh bread) from Heaven, then research this revelation. Research can be an intimate time of worship combining study, praise, contemplative prayer, and intercession. Use this method in both the revelation you receive. Then ask the Father how He would have you serve this revelation to His Body.

29. What wood was primarily used in making the tabernacle furnishings? What prophetic significance did this wood have regarding the furnishings?

30. How does the mercy call manifest in your life?

31. The Altar of Incense reiterates Levi's call to _____ and _____.

32. Which tabernacle furnishings reinforce Levi's call to purity and intimacy?

33. What is the *Maaleh Ashan?* How does it relate to the tribe of Levi today?

34. Meditate on Exodus 25:31–40 and do a deeper study. What is the Lord revealing to you personally?

35. The Ark of the Covenant has special meaning for the tribe of Levi. The _____ were called to carry the _____.

36. How are you a unique carrier of the Glory?

## Journal Activity

In reviewing the section regarding Levi's connection to the tabernacle furnishings in the Outer and Inner Court and the Holy of Holies, what is your intimate love story with Yeshua? How does this love story manifest in your everyday life? As the fragrance of Christ, how does your intimacy with the Bridegroom draw others into intimacy?

**Optional Creative Activity**: Depict what you've journaled through an art expression such as painting, music, dance, or poetry. You may even want to repeat this activity every day for a week, each day a different creative expression.

37. Studying Jacob's prophecy to Simeon and Levi in Genesis 49:5–7, what do you feel could have led to Levi's engagement in the incident? How has anger side-railed you from abiding in perfect love?

38. Take time to dig into the wealth of revelation in Moses' prophecy to the tribe of Levi in Deuteronomy 33:8–11 and complete the following exercises and questions.

    A. Do a word study and research the Thummim and Urim that Moses speaks of in this scripture? What is the Holy Spirit highlighting to you about this mystery?

    B. Read Exodus 17:1–7 and Numbers 20:13. In Hebrew what do the names Massah and Meribah mean?

    C. What is the prophetic significance of Rephidim?

    D. How has the Lord allowed you to be tested?

    E. Like Moses, how have you quarreled against the Lord? What did you learn from these experiences? How have you grown?

F. Who is the rock in Exodus 17:1–7? How have you, in your sin, struck the rock? Where do we see this prophetic parallel in the gospel story?

G. When Moses said, "*Who said of his father and his mother, 'I did not consider them'; and he did not acknowledge his brothers, nor did he regard his own sons, for they observed Your word, and kept Your covenant,*" what was the Lord asking of the Levites?

H. What has your radical obedience cost you in relationships? Ask the Father what He is calling you to surrender now in your life.

I. What deep mysteries has God called you to release to the Body of Christ? How does it relate to your core values, life message, and your intimacy with the Lord?

J. Which portion of Moses' prophecy specifically relates to Levi's call to intercession?

K. What does a life of sacrifice entail for you personally? How does sacrifice bring you deeper into intimacy with Yeshua?

L. What is Levi's substance? How does the Father bless the work of Levi's hands? How does this manifest in your life?

39. Read Numbers 16:1–33. How did Korah fall away from the Lord? What did Korah neglect? How can you learn from Korah's demise?

40. In Psalms how do we see God restore Korah's family line? What contribution did they give to us in Scripture?

41. Eli was so caught up in the work of the ministry—what did he lose sight of? What did it cost him?

42. How have you fallen into the same snares as Eli?

43. What truly grieved the Lord about Nadab and Abihu's offering of strange fire? Why is strange fire so deadly to us spiritually?

44. In his weakness, Uzzah entered into striving and tried to touch the glory of God. How have you engaged in striving in your flesh and gone ahead of the Lord? What consequences occurred? What valuable lesson did you learn? How has the Father redeemed this situation?

45. How have you allowed the leaven of the Pharisees in your life?

46. Where has the spirit of religion disillusioned and deceived you most?

47. In the golden calf incident Aaron compromised because of the fear of man. How has the fear of man detoured your destiny and kept you from walking in your priesthood?

48. What is the difference between the Aaronic priesthood and the Zadok priesthood? How have you operated in both of these? How have you gotten caught in "doing" instead of "being"?

49. What is the deception of performance agendas? What spirit is at work in performance agendas?

50. How does He want to free you from the spirit of religion?

51. Study Levitical forerunners in the Bible, history, and current day, and write about it. What do they have in common? How do you personally identify with them?

52. How does separateness call you into deep union with the Lord?

53. Prophetically speaking, as a modern-day Levite what is your role in the Temple (if it is not made with human hands)?

54. What unique place do Levites hold today in the restoration of the fallen Tabernacle of David?

55. How can you relate to the passion Ezra had for building the Lord's House?

56. In a time of contemplative prayer and worship, study and meditate on Joshua 3:1–17. What is the Lord speaking to you about habitation?

# ACTIVATION EXERCISE

As the Holy Spirit leads, in your own unique expression of your union with Yeshua plan a Jewish wedding ceremony. It does not have to be an elaborate event. It is only important that it be heartfelt, a time of communion and intimacy. Invite others and share your heart and revelation about intimacy with the Lord. Adding live worship to this event would definitely create the atmosphere for everyone to encounter the Lord. You may want to teach or enact this as a drama—just let it come as an act of worship. Keep these thoughts in mind when seeking the Lord to plan this event: What does it mean to be married to Him? What does it mean to be separate unto the Lord? Prepare wedding vows to the Lord. Ask Yeshua what are His wedding vows to you? You may want to ask your guests to do the same. Afterwards, take time to allow your heart to process the event and journal about it.

## 12 Declarations for the Tribe of Levi

1. I am a true WORSHIPER that my Father is seeking for. I WORSHIP my Heavenly Father in Spirit and Truth.

2. I am JOINED to the Lord in holy matrimonial union. NOTHING can separate me from the LOVE of God.

3. As a priest, I can DRAW NEAR to my Bridegroom King and with BOLDNESS enter the holy place.

4. I am one of Yeshua's RARE bridal flowers: PRECIOUS, BEAUTIFUL, FRAGRANT, and COSTLY. I call others into the Garden of the Lord.

5. I am a walking PDA (public display of affection) with my lover. I unapologetically RADIATE INTIMACY with my Groom wherever I go!

6. I am a CARRIER of God's GLORY. The Ark of the Covenant has HABITATION inside of me.

7. My Father has entrusted me with the ORACLES of Heaven. I am a SCRIBE who pens God's mysteries and love letters to men!

8. With REVERENCE and HOLY FEAR, I steward FAITHFULLY the mystery of the *Maaleh Ashan*. My worship and intercession is first and foremost vertical—for an audience of One.

9. My PURITY, SEPERATENESS, and CONSECRATION to God are my greatest weapons.

10. In Yeshua's name I am FREE of the facades of anger, fear of man, performance mindsets, the leaven of the Pharisees, and the spirit of religion. My habitation is HOLY unto my lover Yeshua. I am CHASTE—I am the Lamb's wife! I will FOLLOW Him wherever He goes!

11. I am a forerunner who BURNS with revival fire. Like Ezra, I burn to REBUILD that habitation of the Lord.

12. I carry the cry of HABITATION. As Yeshua's priestly Bride I make a HOME with my Bridegroom.

# Chapter 5

## Judah: The Government of Praise

1. If the Kingdom of God is righteousness, peace, and joy, then what is its government?

2. What are the precepts of the Kingdom built upon?

3. God has ordained that Judah would _____.

4. According to Genesis 29:35 what does Judah's name mean?

5. Judah's existence flounders apart from the _____.

6. What is true praise?

7. In order to truly offer the Lord genuine praise, what must you possess?

8. Praise is _____.

9. When you lay your life down before the Lord, how does this magnify Him?

# Journal Activity

Find your favorite praise and worship music that causes you to ascend into the throneroom. Make it your passionate focus to magnify the Lord, holding nothing back. How can you uniquely express unadulterated praise before the throne of God? Do this every day for one week in your quiet time with the Lord. After each time of worship, journal from your experience. At the end of the week how have you grown as a worshiper? What has transformed in your heart?

10. Study James 1:9 and meditate upon it. Why is this such a vital heart position for Judah?

11. What is the gemstone of Judah?

12. This exquisite gemstone is the intense color of what?

13. In Judah's gemstone we can see Yeshua as who and what?

14. In relation to Judah's gemstone—what color do associate with praise?

15. What else can we associate the gemstone of Judah with?

16. Meditate on Revelation 4:3. What does this mystery reveal?

Taking in the richness of the typology within Judah's gemstone, what does this mean to you personally? How do you see Yeshua as that perfect emerald, the Cornerstone of Abba's house of Living Stones?

**Optional Creative Activity**: Upon this reflection express what you journaled creatively in an artform (painting, singing, dance, poetry, etc.).

17. What is the tribe of Judah's symbol?

18. What are the three stages of maturity found in the tribe of Judah?

19. Reflecting on the early life of King David, how was God training him? What were the lessons he needed to learn?

20. How can you identify with young David in his infancy as a lion cub?

21. What causes many a young Judah to falter?

22. _____ takes a _____ to be developed.

23. What and who is needed for a young Judah's development?

24. What are the pitfalls to the tribe of Judah in their infancy?

25. What takes place in the tribe of Judah's adolescent phase?

26. In King David's adolescent phase as a Judah, what lessons was the Father giving David in His lovingkindness?

27. Judah experiences great growing pains in their adolescent phase. What is the journey of transformation they must pursue, and how can you identify with it in your life?

28. During the adolescent phase the tribe of Judah has an insatiable appetite. What must Judah feast on? How can you have an insatiable appetite for God?

29. What does the Hebrew word *tsaba* mean?

30. When can the Father entrust His Kingdom to Judah?

31. How does a Judah develop his or her roar?

32. Meditate and do a contemplative study on Psalm 104:21–22. What is the Lord revealing to you personally?

33. Referring to the open vision I received (mentioned on pages 75–76): what is the Lord prophetically speaking into your life regarding this revelation?

34. Describe in detail the adulthood phase for the tribe of Judah. How does God want to advance you into maturity? What would that look like in your everyday walk with Him?

35. What must Judah lay down in order to inherit dominion and become the government of praise?

36. Upon maturity the tribe of Judah can make what?

37. According to I Peter 5:8–9, who is the counterfeit lion?

38. When can Judah's spiritual sense of smell wane? How can it be restored?

39. Describe an intimate portrayal of Yeshua, as the Lion of the Tribe of Judah.

40. How is He roaring over you?

41. Study Joel 3:16–17. What does this mean prophetically in this hour?

#  JACOB'S PROPHECY

**The following questions and journal activity coincide with Jacob's prophecy to the tribe of Judah.**

42. Study, contemplate, and dive deep into Jacob's prophecy to Judah in Genesis 49:8–12. Answer what the Lord is speaking prophetically and what it means to you personally.

    A. *"Judah, your brothers shall praise you."*

    B. *"Your hand shall be upon the neck of your enemies."*

C. *"Judah is a lion's whelp; from the prey, My son you have gone up; He couches, He lies down as a lion, and as a lion, who dares rouse him up?"*

D. *"The scepter shall not depart from Judah, nor the rulers staff from between His feet, until Shiloh comes"*

E. *"And to Him shall be the obedience of the peoples."*

F. *"He ties the foal to the vine, and His donkey's colt to the choice vine."*

G. *"He washes His garments in wine, and His robes in the blood of grapes. His eyes are dull from wine, and His teeth white from milk."*

# MOSES' PROPHECY

**The following questions and journal activity coincide with Moses' prophecy to the tribe of Judah.**

43. How does the Lord hear the voice of Judah? Answer honestly, do you feel the Lord hears your voice? If yes, how does He hear you? If no, what lies are you believing that keep you from knowing that the Father hears you?

44. Does your voice matter? Is it a powerful roar or a soft purr of a kitten? Ask the Father what kind of voice has He given you.

45. The tribe of Judah is a company of _____-_____ who know how to _____ the _____ of their _____.

46. What is the two-fold call in this portion of Moses' prophecy: "And bring Him to the obedience of His people"? What does it mean today?

47. As the Lion of Judah, how has the Lord contended for you?

48. What is the Achilles' heel of every Judah? If you are a Judah, how has the Lord helped you overcome this facade?

49. What is the one thing that can separate us from the throneroom?

50. Study Ezekiel 28:12–18. How does Lucifer's fall bring a strong warning to the tribe of Judah? What can you as a worshiper learn from Lucifer's demise? How has some modern-day worship strayed from God's heart from pure unadulterated praise and worship? How can it be restored?

51. What is the difference between horizontal and vertical worship? Which one pleases God's heart?

52. Judah carries the _____ of _____.

53. The spirit of oppression is a common facade in the tribe of Judah, often manifesting in depression, anxiety, laziness, and/or despondency. How have you struggled with the spirit of oppression? How does the Lord deliver you from the spirit of oppression?

54. What facade is a common thread in leadership, especially for this tribe?

55. How did David, Solomon, and others in Scripture struggle with this façade? What lessons did they learn? Who did not learn the lessons of overcoming this facade? Have you struggled from this facade? How have you (or can you) overcome this facade through Christ?

56. According to Matthew 4:8–11, how was Yeshua tempted, yet triumphant?

57. How did God bring redemption through the bloodline of Judah?

58. What can restore Judah's rightful place of dominion and release his true Kingdom authority?

59. What is the cry of consummation? On a personal level what does it mean to you? If you are a Judah, how has the Lord called you to release the cry of consummation in the earth?

60. What does the mystery of the *issur yichud* reveal, and how does it relate to the Millennial Reign of Messiah?

## Judah: The Government of Praise

61. According to Psalm 132:1–5, what was King David's greatest passion? How was it fulfilled and through whom?

62. What tribe also carries a passion for habitation like Judah and builds the Lord's habitation alongside Judah?

63. In I Samuel 23:25 where does David run from Saul (Hebrew name)? What intimate prophetic revelation do you see for yourself in this story?

64. How is God restoring the fallen tabernacle of David today? What is your role in this end-time restoration?

## ACTIVATION EXERCISE

**\*\*\* This activation is for the Tribe of Judah only.**

Seek the Lord in leading a time of worship, whether it be through song, dance, or art. Gleaning what you have learned about your spiritual DNA as a Judah, lead people into the throneroom. How has God transformed you through knowing your unique spiritual DNA? How has it changed you as a worshiper and leader? Journal about your journey as a Judah. Where is the Lord calling you to grow? Where have you grown already? How can you release the cry of consummation in the earth? What does your holy roar sound like?

# 12 Declarations for the Tribe of Judah

1. God has called me to be a POWERFUL INSTRUMENT of PRAISE to minister to Him!

2. THRONEROOM WORSHIP is the core of my spiritual DNA.

3. God has given me a HOLY ROAR! By His Spirit I am called to release it in the earth!

4. I will embrace bowing low as a lifestyle to EXHORT and MAGNIFY the Lord with all my heart.

5. God has given me a mandate to carry the GOVERNMENT of PRAISE in His Kingdom.

6. I AM FIERCER than I know. My worship is POWERFUL! God has appointed me to the frontlines of battle. I intimidate the enemy with my unbridled praise.

7. God has given me the GARMENT of PRAISE for the spirit of heaviness.

8. As I surrender my pride and embrace true brokenness, I will BRILLANTLY SHINE as the exquisite emerald Abba designed me to be.

9. I will GOVERN alongside my Bridegroom King as His FIERCE Lioness Bride.

10. I RUN toward the battle, knowing my authority lies in the POWERFUL PRAISE I ascribe to my Lover Yeshua!

11. God is using me to RAISE UP the fallen Tabernacle of David.

12. God will RESTORE my fortunes and bring me into my full healing. In the beauty of His holy habitation I will FOREVER ABIDE!

# Chapter 6

# Dan: The Voice of Justice

1. _____ and _____ are the foundation of God's throne.

2. When can we find true freedom and justice?

3. What has the Father endowed the tribe of Dan to be?

4. What are some of the vital roles Danites have in the Body of Christ?

5. What is the meaning of Dan's name?

# ACTIVATION EXERCISE

What areas do you most need to see justice for in your personal life? Make a petition for justice accordingly. In a time of worship and prayer, ask the Lord to take you to the courts of Heaven. Present your petition to the Father, the Great Judge. How do you see Yeshua, your mediator? What is Abba's ruling? What areas is He bringing a cease and desist order in your life? List at least five decrees of justice. This is your legal document binding in Heaven and earth. Make these decrees for the next week. Journal about the deep work the Lord did in your life in the courts of Heaven.

6. Genesis 30:6 talks about Dan's birth. What took place spiritually during the time of his birth, and how would it form his nature? How can you relate to Dan's birth in the story of your own life?

7. The gemstone for Dan is the _____.

8. What two things has this gemstone been connected to? How do you feel this speaks to you?

9. The Ten Commandments, according to the Talmud, were written upon what?

## Journal Activity

In Exodus 24:10–18 the children of Israel encounter one of the strongest manifestations of God's glory. As you meditate on what occurred, turn on some soaking music and picture yourself there, as one of the children of Israel. What is God revealing to you?

**Optional Creative Activity**: In a painting, express the above revelation and how you encountered the Lord.

## JACOB'S PROPHECY

*"Dan shall judge his people, as one of the tribes of Israel. Dan shall be a serpent in the way, a horned snake in the path, that bites the horse's heels, so his rider falls backward. For Thy salvation I wait, O Lord."* (Genesis 49:16–18).

**The following questions and journal activity coincide with Jacob's prophecy to the tribe of Dan.**

10. According to Genesis 49:16–18, what is Dan called to do as one of the twelve tribes of Israel?

11. The Father's heart is always to have _____ triumph over _____.

12. Study and meditate on Judges 2:11–17. In verses 16–18, Israel cried out to the Lord for deliverance. How did God answer them?

13. How does justice relate to intimacy?

14. How has God's justice triumphed over the enemy in your life?

Contemplate God's heart of justice. How has justice brought you restoration, vindication, and restored communion with the Father? How do you passionately burn for justice? Has God called you to be a deliverer, a minister of reconciliation, and a voice of justice?

15. What is the tribe of Dan's driving passion?

16. Jacob prophesied over his son Dan:

    *"Dan shall be a serpent in the way, a horned snake in the path, that bites the horse's heels, so his rider falls backwards."*

    What was God speaking to the tribe of Dan's about their strengths and weaknesses? Do you relate to Dan's strengths and weaknesses? If so, how?

17. Dan has very keen _____ and can rightly divide truth when _____ to God.

18. Why do Danites make powerful counselors and deliverance ministers?

19. How can Dan's cunning nature cause him to wound others?

20. How do you see Yeshua as your knight in shining armor? Where has hope deferred blinded you from seeing the salvation of the Lord in your circumstances?

# MOSES' PROPHECY

*And of Dan he said, "Dan is a lion's whelp that leaps forth from Bashan," * Deuteronomy 33:22

**The following questions and journal activity coincide with Moses' prophecy to the tribe of Dan.**

21. When Moses prophesied to the tribe of Dan: *"Dan is a lion's whelp,"* how was he referring to Dan's immaturity?

22. How was Dan portraying a role given to Him by God? Have you ever tried to be someone you are not? How did this disillusion you and cause you pain?

23. How does Dan's misinterpretation, or copycatting Judah, stem from an anti-Christ spirit? What is God's heart of redemption for Dan?

24. What does it mean to "take on" the Spirit of Christ?

25. How do you feel I Peter 4:12–13 is a commission for the tribe of Dan?

26. According to Moses' prophecy, how does Bashan serve as a warning for the tribe of Dan? How have you leaped into things prematurely?

27. Samson's colorful life was full of highs and lows. How do you identify with his strengths and weaknesses?

28. Samson was born from a barren woman. Ask the Holy Spirit how the Father longs to birth justice from barren places in your life. Write below.

29. *Manoah,* meaning "rest" in Hebrew, was Samson's father. How can you find justice in the rest of the Lord?

30. What is the Nazarite vow according to Scripture? How did Samson keep this vow? How did he break his Nazarite vow? How can we as believers symbolically keep a Nazarite vow today?

31. How is Dan an unconventional deliverer?

32. How can idolatry keep you from sidestepping your destiny? If you have, what is the Holy Spirit's counsel for a course correction?

33. Samson lost his _____ _____ long before he lost it in the natural.

34. Read Leviticus 24:10–16, 23. How can the tongue serve as a weapon of warfare and freedom for Dan? How can it serve as the implement of death for the tribe of Dan?

## Journal Activity

Study and meditate on James 3:2–11 and Isaiah 6:5–7. How is the Lord speaking to you to tame your tongue? Ask Him for a revelation of His glory like Isaiah had. How can He use you to be a voice of justice in the earth?

## Living Stones Study Guide

35. Read Joshua 19:40–48. What is the seventh lot? What significance does it have for the tribe of Dan?

36. Read Judges 1:34. Why did the Amorites overtake the tribe of Dan and cause them to forego their inheritance? In what areas of your life have you allowed the enemy to overtake you and compromise your inheritance? How does the Lord want to restore your inheritance?

37. What is the strongman spoken of in Matthew 12:29, 43–45? How can you overcome the strongman in your own life?

38. According to Judges 18, how did the tribe of Dan settle for less than they were created for? What can you personally glean from this story?

## ACTIVATION EXERCISE

In a time of worship ask the Lord to take you to the Council Room of Heaven. Ask Him for strategies and counsel of wisdom for your life. Make a Council Board from what He reveals to you. Include strategies to overcome areas in which you have been stuck in your life. As you obtain victory and grow, document the follow-through of your progress and journal.

39. Have you (past or present) judged yourself unworthy to worship? What lies do you believe? What truth is Abba revealing to combat the lie and overcome it?

40. Every Dan goes through intense refinement in the Father's molting process. How have you been through a molting process? What lessons are the most vital to you in the molting process?

41. What was the tribe of Dan's contribution to the building of the Tabernacle?

**\*\*\*FOR THE TRIBE OF DAN ONLY**

Abba is the Master Craftsman. Ask Him for a download of a creative project as a co-creator with Him. How can you adorn His house? How can creativity reflect God's heart for justice? Let your project reflect this, and have fun!

# 12 Declarations for the Tribe of Dan

1. God has called me to be a POWERFUL VOICE of JUSTICE in the earth. I am as wise as a serpent and harmless as a dove.

2. As I walk according to the laws and precepts of my Father's heart,

3. My Father has called me to KNOW the MYSTERIES of His throne and REVEAL them in the earth.

4. I am CONSECRATED with a Nazarite vow. My STERNGTH comes from the Lord alone.

5. I carry the scales of justice, BALANCING them in MERCY and RIGHTOUSNESS.

6. God has given me His holy law, which comes from His sapphire throne. As I SURRENDER my own false judgements of myself and others, He releases His RIGHTOUS JUDGEMENTS to me.

7. I will BOLDY DECREE Abba's righteous judgments without partiality, pride, or fear.

8. Restoring justice is my INHERITANCE as a son of God. FREEDOM and RESTORATION are anthems I shall sing eternally.

9. I am a mature eagle who WAITS upon the Lord. He RENEWS my STERNGTH and has called me to SOAR in the heights of His love.

10. As I bridle my tongue to bring RESTORATION, to BUILD and not tear down. I will DEFEND the poor and decree righteousness and deliverance to the captives.

11. God has APPOIONTED me to the Courtroom of Heaven. I OVERTURN Satan's faulty schemes, call for cease and desist orders to all injustice, DECREE my Father's righteous orders, and issue RECOMPENSE to His saints.

12. As a skillful master craftsman Abba has called me to ADORN His house. I am a CO-CREATOR with my Father, and He has given me His blueprints and strategies to restore His holy habitation.

# Chapter 7

## Naphtali: The Doe Set Free!

1. What passion did God ordain the tribe of Naphtali to carry?

2. What does the name of Naphtali mean?

3. What prophetic implications of Naphtali's birth are painted in Scripture?

4. Meditating on Ephesians 6:12, how does Scripture define spiritual warfare?

5. How have you engaged in warfare in the flesh (striving), and how you have wrestled in the Spirit? What is the difference? What fruit is produced from warring in the flesh versus the Spirit?

6. How can striving be a detour to destiny? Where have you personally experienced detours from striving in your flesh?

7. What faux pas do intercessors and deliverance ministers need to be aware of to avoid in ministry?

8. Read Revelation 2:20–23. How do we tolerate the spirit of control and open ourselves up to all kinds of idol worship, sickness, mind control, and witchcraft?

9. What spirit seeks to usurp true authority and dominion of a believer?

10. What spiritual abuses have you seen in the Church, and how has this affected you personally?

11. To demean someone's _____ and _____ is to demean Creation of God's _____ within them.

12. True spiritual authority is becoming whom we truly are in Christ, serving the Lord and one another in love and humility in the fullness of our dominion. How can you walk this truth out in your own life, and how can you edify your brothers and sisters in Messiah to do the same?

13. When you feel tempted to strive, engage in perfectionism and control, what can you do to avoid this snare?

# ACTIVATION EXERCISE

Exhortation Exercise: Create multiple copies of every tribe's gemstone using craft paper, leaving a space in the center to write upon. Identify the tribe of each person in your small circle of faith (5–15 people for example). Create a board with their picture. In a quiet time with the Lord, ask Him what facets of the Father (according to their tribe) He sees in them. One by one, edify each person in their identity, gifts, and callings, writing these traits upon their gemstone. Commit to see each one as the Father does and declare how you will partner with the Lord and them to come into the fullness of who they are and their destiny. Repent to them where you have falsely judged them or failed to encourage them. You may even want to encourage them do this exercise also! Process and journal about this experience. What did you learn from this experience? How were you transformed? How did this activity build a closer bond in the Spirit with your spiritual family? What transformation and growth occurred in them?

Naphtali: The Doe Set Free!

14. What is the gemstone for the tribe of Naphtali?

15. What characteristics of Naphtali's strength does this gemstone speak to? What characteristics within this gemstone speak of this tribe's weaknesses?

16. If you are from the tribe of Naphtali, what is the Father speaking to you regarding the beauty inside you? What facades flaw this beauty?

17. The calling of an intercessor has a definite correlation with spiritual birthing. This is most dominant within the tribe of Naphtali. What has God called you to birth? How can you partner with Heaven in the birthing of sons and daughters in the Earth?

18. Upon hearing the Word of the Lord, what will the tribe of Naphtali do?

19. Define the apostolic nature in which Naphtali builds the Father's Kingdom. If you are from the tribe of Naphtali, how does this manifest in your own life and calling?

## Journal Activity

Meditate on Romans 8:19–25. Discuss with Holy Spirit about what truly is the groaning mentioned in Romans 8. Express how you feel it manifests. How can you partner with Abba to see the revealing of His sons and daughters?

20. Meditate on the following:

   *As the deer pants for the water books, so my soul pants for Thee, O God. My soul thirsts for God, for the living God.* (Psalm 42:1–2)

   How do you see this as a picture of intimacy?

21. How is the symbol of the deer poignant for the tribe of Naphtali?

## JACOB'S PROPHECY

*Naphtali is a doe let loose; He gives beautiful words.* **(Genesis 49:21)**

*Naphtali is a doe let loose that bears beautiful fawns.* **(KJV)**

**The following questions and journal activity coincide with Jacob's prophecy to the tribe of Naphtali.**

22. Jacob's prophecy speaks of Naphtali's call to _____.

23. The deer has no gallbladder. Prophetically this speaks to Naphtali to not hold on to any guile or bitterness. How has holding on to guile and bitterness hindered your walk with the Lord? How has it kept you from unconditionally loving others as Yeshua does?

24. What truth can you arm yourself with to guard against bitterness?

25. What was Jacob's prophecy speaking of when he said, "Naphtali gives beautiful words" or "bears beautiful fawns"?

26. Jacob's prophecy also speaks of Naphtali's calling to _____ and _____.

## MOSES' PROPHECY

*And of Naphtali he said, "O Naphtali, satisfied with favor, And full of the blessing of the Lord, take possession of the sea and the south." (Deuteronomy 33:23)*

**The following questions and journal activity coincide with Jacob's prophecy to the tribe of Naphtali.**

27. Wherever there is liberty, there is _____ and _____.

28. How can walking in fullness of who you are from a place of intimacy bring favor to your life?

29. What was the Lord speaking to the tribe of Naphtali when He said, "take possession of the sea and the south"?

## Journal Activity

Naphtali, alongside the tribe of Zebulun, inherited the Galilee region. Do a word study of Yeshua's ministry in the Galilee. What do you hear Him speaking to you as a Naphtali (or to and through the tribe of Naphtali)? Keep in mind Naphtali's nature and calling. What ultimately is Father's nature revealed through Naphtali's inheritance in the Galilee?

30. Why does Satan seek to hunt, capture, and destroy Naphtali?

31. Like the deer the tribe of Naphtali can be ensnared by the façade of fear. What are the two ways the enemy can use this façade against Naphtali?

    A)

    B)

**\*\*\*For the tribe of Naphtali only.**

Read *Hinds Feet on High Places* by Hannah Hurnard, seeing yourself in the footsteps of the main character, *Much Afraid*. As you read, note and journal your own snares of fear and intimidation, where you have felt unworthy, unloved, and rejected. Make a map starting at the Valley of Humiliation and ending in the High Places. Note each triumph, detour, and discovery on this beautiful adventure of freedom with the Beloved *Shepherd King*. Be creative and have fun! At the end share your testimony of transformation with fellow believers, using the map you've created. Invite them to take the same journey.

32. What are two common snares for leadership in ministry?

33. What must Naphtali learn to do as a spiritual father or mother?

34. How have abuses in leadership wounded the Body? How have unhealthy leaders wounded you personally? Have you ever crossed the line and used tactics of control and intimidation yourself?

35. How has the spirit of abortion robbed your own life?

36. Read Judges 4 and 5. How did Barack's shortcomings detour him and potentially abort his Kingdom mandate?

37. How can you identify with Barack?

38. The tribes of Naphtali and Zebulun are an unstoppable Kingdom duo. If you are from either of these tribes, how has the other tribe contributed to your growth, been a bulwark of strength, and how has the Father called you to partner with them?

39. How did Tabitha (Dorcus) in the New Testament embody the tribe of Naphtali, and how can you relate to her today?

40. How is the Lord calling you as a liberator? A repairer of the breach? A minister of reconciliation?

# 12 Declarations for the Tribe of Naphtali

1. I am a doe set FREE! The VICTORY Yeshua paid for me brings me ETERNAL LIBERTY!

2. I am a BRILLANT diamond who SHINES in the darkness! I am a BEAUTY BEARER of the Kingdom who attracts many to the King.

3. I am Abba's of-the-box DELIVERER! When SURRENDERED to the Holy Spirit, I am UNSTOPPABLE!

4. I do not WRESTLE with flesh and blood. The weapons of my warfare are MIGHTY, to pull down strongholds in heavenly places.

5. Fear has NO PLACE in me. I am a POWERFULL conduit of UNCONDITIONAL LOVE. I have a SOUND MIND that knows the counsels of my Father.

6. God has called me BIRTH His sons and daughters. I take my place in the birthing room of Heaven.

7. I am CAPTIVATED by Love Divine Himself, and He is captivated by beautiful surrender to Him!

8. Abba has given me His counsels to NURTURE, TRAIN, and RAISE UP His end-time army.

9. EVERYTING the Lord has spiritually impregnated me with will come to a healthy and glorious birthing! NOTHING will be aborted, miscarried, or stillborn in Yeshua's name!

10. I DEFY boxes of religion, man-made agendas, and formulas. I BIRTH and CREATE with the Father from a place of intimacy, freedom, and surrender.

11. I give BIRTH in His holy sanctuary, Kadesh. Everything within me cries HOLY!

12. What once were obstacles I used to fear have now become mountains I JOYFULLY LEAP over with my Beloved!

# Chapter 8

## Gad: The Habitation of God's Fortune

1. _____ is a revealing of _____: God to us and whom we truly are in Him.

2. What have you learned thus far on your own journey of habitation with the Lord?

3. What do the characteristics (A–E) of Gad's name mean, and how do you relate to them?

    A. Fortunate:

    B. Fortune:

    C. Invade:

    D. Overcome:

    E. Troop:

4. What is the gemstone for the tribe of Gad?

5. How does Gad's gemstone speak of habitation?

# ACTIVATION EXERCISE

In your quiet time alone with the Lord, bask in His majesty under the stars at night for a week while meditating on Psalm 8:1–5. Consider the frailty of your own humanity. How does the Father invite you to partake of His majestic glory?

 ***Optional Creative exercise: Respond to this exercise in an art form such as writing, drawing, painting, dancing, playing music, etc.

6. How have lies, mistakes of the past, and insecurities kept you earthbound rather than the citizen of Heaven you truly are?

7. What does being a citizen of Heaven mean to you? How can you walk this out in your everyday life?

8. The _____ nature of Gad defines his life and ministry.

9. Gad's tribal symbol is three tents. How does it represent the Cross, and what is the Lord calling the tribe to see in themselves? What do Gads carry in this revelation to others?

# Journal Activity

The tribe of Gad is known for their wandering nature, which speaks of their folly and their lifelong journey into habitation. How have you been a wanderer? Where has wandering brought you pain because of bad choices and toxic beliefs? How has wandering given you the vantage point of seeing the beauty of the temporal life and your eternal home?

10. What happens when Gad ceases from his wandering and settles in his rightful inheritance of habitation?

##  JACOB'S PROPHECY

*"As for Gad, raiders shall raid him, but he shall raid at their heels."*
(Genesis 49:19)

**The following questions and journal activity coincide with Jacob's prophecy to the tribe of Gad.**

11. When Jacob prophesied, "raiders shall raid him," what was the Lord saying to this tribe, and how do you identify with this personally in your life?

12. What God-given gift does the enemy seek to destroy in Gad?

13. The Lord turns the tables on the enemy, when Jacob prophesies, "but he shall raid at their heels." How is the Lord calling you to raid the enemy?

14. How has He taken a previous situation where you were bombarded by the enemy and turned it around so you were bombarding the enemy?

15. What transformation occurred in you because of this, and what did you learn?

## MOSES' PROPHECY

*And of Gad he said, "Blessed is the one who enlarges Gad; he lies down as a lion, and tears the arm, also the crown of the head. Then he provided the first part for himself, for there the ruler's portion was reserved; and he came with the leaders of the people; he executed the justice of the Lord, and His ordinances with Israel."*
(Deuteronomy 33:20–21)

**The following questions and journal activity coincide with Moses' prophecy to the tribe of Gad.**

16. What do you feel the Lord was saying when Moses prophesied, "Blessed is the one who enlarges Gad." How has the Lord enlarged you?

17. What revelation will cause Gad to be enlarged?

18. What does this portion of the prophecy speak of: "he lies down as a lion, and tears the arm, also the crown of the head"?

19. What warfare strategies have been most effective for you personally?

20. Gad is a chameleon and can mimic other tribes. How has insecurity displaced your identity and caused you to blend in rather than stand out? Why do you (and /or others) hide who truly are?

21. Read I Chronicles 12:8, 14–15. The tribe's fierce, warlike nature caught the attention of King David. How did the tribe of Gad demonstrate Moses' prophecy? If you are from the tribe of Gad, how do you see yourself in this prophecy?

22. "He lies down as a lion," prophesies a two-fold meaning for the tribe of Gad.

    A. How does Gad "lying down as a lion" speak of entering to rest and habitation?

    B. In reference to Numbers 32:6–9, how does Gad become lazy like a lion?

23. How has resting in the Lord during warfare caused you to grow?

24. How has trauma and striving caused you to settle and become lazy?

25. How does the tribe of Gad tear the arm of their enemies?

26. When Moses prophesied, *"also the crown of the head,"* how can we as believers take down the crown from Satan's head?

Moses prophesied, "Then he provided the first part for himself," speaking of how Gad settled on the wrong side of the Jordan. How have you settled for less than you were created for? What can you do to stop settling?

27. What prophetic gift does Gad mirror in the tribe of Dan?

28. What are the three idols of the heart that can detour Gad from habitation?

29. How can the appetite of the flesh cause us to wander?

30. How have you gorged yourself on spiritual junk food and become malnourished?

31. What should you feast on instead?

## ACTIVATION EXERCISE

Hold a feast. On one side of the table set with beautiful linens and china as well as nourishing and healthy cuisine. On the opposite side of the table place plastic tablecloth, paper plates, and all manner of "junk food." Delve into the revelation of the fruits of the Spirit verses the malnourishment of spiritual junk food we desire. Get input from each person the difference between the two and why we go after unhealthy things of the flesh verses things of the Sprit. How can we remain steadfast and feast only at the Lord's table? What keys did you learn from this exercise?

32. How has a sedentary or lazy spirit detoured you into foreign pastures? What truth will break this cycle from reoccurring?

33. How can Gad lay out the welcome mat for lying spirits and divination?

34. How have you seen this lead to grave delusion in your life or others?

35. The infantile wanderings of Gad are likened unto those of the prodigal son. Read Luke 15:13–24. How do see yourself in this story?

36. How did the Father later redeem Gad's wandering and settling on the wrong side of the Jordan?

37. How did the prophet Elijah demonstrate the strengths and weaknesses of Gad?

38. How do you identify with Elijah?

39. The prophet Elijah carried an evangelistic prophetic mantle. How did he display this?

40. How do you see prophetic evangelism demonstrated in the Kingdom today?

 ACTIVATION EXERCISE

Seek the Holy Spirit for a creative way to engage in prophetic evangelism. Organize a team. Debrief with the team afterwards. What did the Lord highlight to you and your team? How did this experience transform you?

41. After Elijah's confrontation with Jezebel, he fled in fear for his life. How has intimidation caused you to wander like Elijah? How have you doubted your own greatness (Abba's nature) within yourself and compromised? List three scriptures that debunk the lie of intimidation and affirm your identity. Make these scriptures declarations for the next two weeks.

## Journal Activity

Meditate on Isaiah 33:20–24. How is the Father asking you to join Him in habitation? How can you partner with the Holy Spirit so that your stakes will not be pulled up and your tent never folded again?

# 12 Declarations for the Tribe of Gad

1. I am a glorious HABITATION OF GOD'S FORTUNE!

2. God has made me FOTUNATE. I am a display of His unmerited favor.

3. My FORTUNE lies in the nature of my Father and His infinite wisdom.

4. God has given me heavenly strategies to INVADE the enemy!

5. I have the supernatural DNA of an unstoppable OVERCOMER!

6. I am a warrior enlisted in a fierce TROOP that overthrows Satan's schemes!

7. I will not allow self-doubt, intimidation, and insecurity to keep me in a cave. I WILL POSSESS my destiny!

8. I possess relentless FAITH! Nothing is impossible with God. As I partner with Him, the miraculous becomes my everyday existence!

9. I am a VITAL and MUCH-LOVED member of God's family! I am no outsider!

10. I refuse to wander and settle for less than I was created for. My ROOTS RUN DEEP into the nature of Christ.

11. I BURN for the restoration of sons to return to the hearts of their fathers.

12. My tent pegs are driven deep into Abba's nature. HEAVEN is my home!

# Chapter 9

## Asher: The Spring of Joy

1. What is a Kingdom principle?

2. _____ is the exact representation of the Father's _____.

3. Meditate on the beauty of John 10:10. How has Yeshua brought you abundant life?

4. The sons of Korah wrote in Psalm 87:7, "*All my springs of joy are in you.*" How have you found your springs of joy in the Lord?

5. _____ longs, _____ and exists for the _____ of the Lord.

6. What propels and sustains the tribe of Asher? How has this been true in your own journey?

7. What does the tribe of Asher impart from the springs of joy in them?

8. A _____ is a natural resource within the _____ that brings life-giving substance.

9. Asherites are gifted with a special empowerment through the joy of the Lord to bring what to the Body?

10. Asher is the eighth son of Jacob. What does this mean prophetically?

11. The _____ of the Lord is the _____ of the work of perfect _____ within our hearts.

12. What is the tribe of Asher strategically planted for in the end times?

13. How do you see the Father using Asher in this way?

14. If you are from the tribe of Asher, what has the Father planted in you to carry out this Kingdom mandate?

Meditate upon the following scripture,

> Then he said to them, "Go, eat of the fat, drink of the sweet, and send portions to him who has nothing prepared; for this day is holy to our Lord, Do not be grieved, for the joy of the Lord is your strength." (Nehemiah 8:10)

How does the joy of the Lord bring you nourishment? How has the joy of the Lord sustained you?

15. What does the name Asher mean?

16. Do a word study on *joy*. Reflect on the wealth of joy the Father has given you.

17. Who are your heroes of faith that exhibit the joy of the Lord, and why?

18. Why do you feel joy is a building block of the Kingdom?

## ACTIVATION EXERCISE

Hold a "Bliss Party" celebrating the joy of the Lord with friends. Break chains of depression, worry, fear, and false burdens off of each other. Have fun and get creative! Abba is always throwing a party in Heaven! Ask Him how you can join Him in it with your Bliss Party.

19. What is Asher's gemstone?

20. How is their gemstone formed, and what does this speak to you personally?

21. The earth tone colors within Asher's gemstone speak of their call to the earth. What revelations has the Father called you to release in the earth?

22. What do you feel is the essence of your Kingdom mandate to release in the earth?

23. What two principles is Creation founded upon?

24. Why are these two principles so vital?

25. List attributes of the tribe of Asher, being one of the most people-oriented tribes, below. In light of this, why is the tribe of Asher so vital? If you are from the tribe of Asher, how do you feel you mirror the Father in these attributes?

# Journal Activity

Speaking of the agate, it is the intense heat of volcanic lava (suffering) that builds the layers and character of Asher. Suffering with each trial forms each band of glory and joy within Asher. How has the Lord used the anvil of suffering in your life? How has this testimony brought Him glory? How did the suffering produce joy in your life?

26. Meditate on Psalm 84:5–7, How has the Lord turned your Valley of Baca into springs of joy?

27. There are _____ of _____ pregnant with joy and anointing that Asher unleashes.

28. How can you allow the enduring work of joy to have full reign in your life?

29. The olive tree (and its components) holds a plethora of meaning for Asher. Dig deep into the meaning of Asher's symbol and how it applies to your life.

    A. The olive tree:

    B. Olives, the fruit of joy:

    C. Olive oil, the outpouring of the Holy Spirit:

# Journal Activity

Gethsemane means "olive press" in Hebrew. When Yeshua was in the Garden of Gethsemane, likewise, he was pressed in a spiritual olive press. For the joy set before Him, Yeshua endured and drank the cup of the Father's will. What has been your Gethsemane experience? How were you transformed? What fruit was produced from this place of suffering?

# JACOB'S PROPHECY

*"As for Asher, his food shall be rich, and he shall yield royal dainties."* (Genesis 49:20)

**The following questions and activation activity coincide with Jacob's prophecy to the tribe of Asher.**

30. What golden manna have you partaken of that drastically changed your life?

31. What rich revelations has the Father called you to serve at His banqueting table?

32. Your _____ is to do the _____ of the Father.

33. Jacob prophesied, *"he shall yield royal dainties,"* representing Asher's call to nourish the Body of Christ with the revelation that they receive from the Father. What two giftings do we see manifested within Asher in this portion of prophecy?

34. What is Asher's teaching ministry centered on?

# ACTIVATION EXERCISE

Hold a banquet with a spread of artisan breads and royal delicacies complete with table finery in an intimate setting of friends. Have all the food represent a prophetic word of affirmation or teaching to each individual. Journal about the experience.

35. When have you partaken of stale bread (revelation)? What effect did this have on your walk with the Lord?

36. How does this prophecy speak of Asher's giving nature?

37. What is a true joyful giver?

38. How can you be more of a joyful giver?

# MOSES' PROPHECY

*And of Asher he said, "More blessed than sons is Asher; May he be favored by his brothers, and may he dip his foot in oil. Your locks shall be iron and bronze, and according to your days, so shall your leisurely walk be." (Deuteronomy 33:24–25)*

*And of Asher he said, Let Asher be blessed with children; let him be acceptable to his brethren, and let him dip his foot in oil. Thy shoes shall be iron and brass; and as thy days, so shall thy strength be. (Deuteronomy 33:24–25)*

**The following questions and journal activity coincide with Moses' prophecy to the tribe of Asher.**

39. Joy is the abundance of what?

40. How do you feel blessing(s) can be derived from joy?

41. Ashers are known for their optimistic, happy-go-lucky personality. How can you partner with Holy Spirit to shift atmospheres?

42. If you are an Asher, how has the Lord endowed you with favor? How has this brought you transformation? How do you impart transformation through the favor of God on your life?

43. Wisdom will give Asher the _____ and _____ to his life.

44. Moses prophesied, "*may he dip his foot in oil."*, How is the anointing Asher's direct tie to the earth?

45. List the difference in experiences when you truly walked in the anointing and when you got caught up in hype and compromised.

46. What is your authentic expression in the anointing?

47. Read Ephesians 5:8–16. What does walking in the anointing truly mean?

# Journal Activity

Read and meditate on Zechariah 4. Picture yourself there like Zechariah, encountering the Lord. Zechariah had a powerful encounter in heavenly places when he saw the lampstand (menorah). In verse 6, he is charged not to live by might nor power of his own, but by the Spirit of the Lord. How can you truly live the Spirit-led life from a day-to-day encounter in His presence? Journal on your encounter(s).

48. How do the two olive trees in Zechariah Chapter 4 represent the Jew and Gentile? Dig deep into this mystery—what does this mean for us today? How is the Holy Spirit inviting you to partner with the Father in this revelation?

49. Moses' prophecy concerning Asher's iron and bronze locks, shoes, and gates, has a two-fold meaning. In your own words explain this and how you relate to the two-fold meaning.

50. What causes Asher to indulge in idolatry?

51. How have you avoided confrontation, and how has this stunted your growth in the Lord?

52. What do you feel is the difference between the pursuit of happiness versus abiding in the fruit of joy?

53. How has a failure to confront kept you from possessing your destiny? Why do you avoid confrontation?

54. How can you stop people pleasing and live for Abba's pleasure?

55. Describe Asher's role in the New Testament. What is the Lord revealing to you?

56. How is the tribe of Asher connected to the Temple? How do you identify with it?

# Journal Activity

How does the Lord want to release deep chasms of joy in and through you? How can you continually abide and cultivate joy?

# 12 Declarations for the Tribe of Asher

1. All my SPRINGS of JOY are in You, Lord!

2. I am the blissful RADIANCE of my Father. I bring Him incredible DELIGHT!

3. Eternal SPRINGS OF JOY are in my innermost being.

4. I am a DEEP SOURCE of anointing that supplies Abba's Kingdom.

5. When the anvil of suffering is applied, I gleefully reply, IT IS WELL with my soul, Abba have your way in me!

6. I am the very CELEBRATION of Heaven in human form. When Heaven throws a party, I am there!

7. I embrace Abba's Gethsemane for me. Pressed in on every side, I choose to ENDURE for the joy set before me.

8. As I share in His sufferings, I know that I also share in His GLORY!

9. Comfort zones will not keep me complacent and avoiding my destiny anymore! I pursue FREEDOM and EVERLASTING JOY in my Beloved.

10. I ABIDE in joy! I am a cultivator of deep wells of anointing.

11. Abba has called me to serve fresh hot bread from the ovens of Heaven. I serve a feast of DEEP REVELATION to His children.

12. Like the prophetess Anna, I abide FAITHFULLY in His Temple and intercede for His people.

# Chapter 10

## Issachar: The Humble Burden Bearer

1. Meditating on Psalm 68:19, how has the Lord born your burdens and brought you salvation?

2. How does the Father call you to walk in His rest and delight?

3. What is one key that will help you enter into the fullness of the Kingdom?

4. The frailty of the _____ nature is to _____, as Adam and Eve did in the Garden.

5. How has striving separated you from intimacy with the Father?

## Journal Activity

Read Isaiah 53:1–5, 12. The Father in His great love and compassion sent to us a humble burden bearer, our Beloved. How do you see Yeshua as the suffering servant in your own life?

6. Define the Hebrew word *nasa* or *nacah*.

7. How does Yeshua embody this for you?

8. The concept of bowing low is a vital Kingdom principle we all must seek to live out. In order to do so, what must you lay down? What must you lift up?

9. What is the calling of every Issachar that Yeshua bore so well?

10. Divine _____ and _____ are both built on the concept of bowing low, for with humility comes honor and elevation from our Father.

11. How can you implement the Kingdom principle of bowing low in your life?

12. What gifting(s) and offices does the tribe of Issachar hold?

13. What does every Issachar know that the true meaning of servanthood is based upon?

## Issachar: The Humble Burden Bearer

14. How has servanthood become distorted? Has it affected your personally? If so, explain.

15. What does Issachar's name mean?

16. Study Genesis 30:14–18. How did the circumstances that surround Issachar's conception form his identity?

17. How have you seen Yeshua as your Baali and your Isshi? What is the difference?

## ACTIVATION EXERCISE

In your worship time make seven declarations of who Yeshua is as your Isshi. Seek the Holy Spirit about how you can apply these declarations as truth to your everyday experience.

18. The connotation of the word *husband* is often tied with the "breadwinner" or the "wage earner" for the family. Meditating on Romans 6:22–23, how is Yeshua your breadwinner?

19. Meditating on Isaiah 40:10, how does the Lord lavish his reward upon Issachar? How have you seen this manifest in your own life?

20. What profound significance does Issachar's conception have because it occurred during the wheat harvest?

21. Why did Abba ordain that Issachar camp with Judah?

22. The gemstone of Issachar is the amethyst. What is the Hebrew name for this gemstone and its prophetic significance?

23. How can the amethyst relate to the fear of the Lord?

Meditate on this Scripture:

*"Blessed are the poor in Spirit, for theirs is the Kingdom of heaven."* (Matthew 5:3)

How do you see Yeshua's message in this scripture resonate the Kingdom principle of bowing low? What other messages did He give on humility in Scripture? How can you relate to His nature of humility? What can you do to be more like Yeshua as the selfless servant?

# ACTIVATION EXERCISE

Seek the Holy Spirit in hosting a small intimate gathering (at least two people and yourself) where you facilitate a foot washing. Gather a basin and towel, anointing oils (optional), and some soft instrumental or soaking music. Wash one another's feet. Ask how you can serve them well as family. Journal about the experience.

24. How can leadership wane and become profaned? What must a true minister/leader do to avoid this?

25. The _____ is the symbol for the tribe of Issachar. This is often referred to as the "_____ _____."

26. Describe the unashamed workman mentioned in II Timothy 2:15. How does the tribe of Issachar especially embody the identity of the unashamed workman? If you are an Issachar, how do you reflect being an unashamed workman in the Kingdom personally?

27. What kind of approach does an Issachar take in his or her prophetic gifting?

28. How can stubbornness taint Issachar's prophetic gifting? How has it hindered you?

29. Describe how Issachar's symbol of the donkey, especially pertaining to the ears and the bray of a donkey, work in the office of the prophet?

30. How has the symbol of the donkey been misunderstood or become cliché in prophetic circles? What revelation will help us to avoid this and see an Issachar for who he or she truly is in Christ?

31. How have you misjudged your own prophetic gifting? What do you feel is the root of your misjudgment?

32. How is the donkey a symbol of majesty for the tribe of Issachar?

33. What workloads has the Father ordained you to carry in your Kingdom mandate?

## Journal Activity

Read Matthew 21:1–11. Yeshua made his triumphant entry as King in humility. During a time of worship picture this scene. What most strikes you about Yeshua as He is riding upon the donkey? How do see yourself in the donkey? Is there a correlation between them? Journal about how you encounter the Lord in this exercise.

***Optional Creative Activity:** In an art form (music, art, poetry, etc.) express the nature and demeanor of Yeshua and the donkey he is riding on.

34. Why is there a dire need for restoration of true servanthood within the Body today?

35. How have abuses of authority in the Church affected you?

*"Issachar is a strong donkey, lying down between the sheepfolds. When he saw that a resting place was good, and the land was pleasant, he bowed his shoulder to bear burdens, and became a slave at forced labor."* (Genesis 49:14–15)

**The following questions with Jacob's prophecy to the tribe of Issachar.**

36. Meditate on II Corinthians 12:9–10. How has your own self-sufficiency hindered you?

37. How can His strength be perfected in your weakness?

38. How has your will (at times) become contrary to the will of the Father, and why?

39. What is the seal of dominion and claim to the inheritance of God's glory on an Issachar's life?

40. Describe the two-fold meaning of this portion of Jacob's prophecy to his son Issachar: "*lying down between the sheepfolds.*" If you are an Issachar, how do you see yourself in this revelation?

41. _____ is a willingness to _____ to our will and _____ in perfect love.

42. How can neglecting to rest in the Lord cause a misguided sense of direction or even false prophecy?

43. What burden of the Lord are you called to carry?

44. How has the Lord called you to bear the burdens of others?

45. Have you ever had a situation where you were submitted to forced labor and been spiritually abused? How has the Lord brought healing to that situation? How can you avoid this in the future?

Issachar: The Humble Burden Bearer

# MOSES' PROPHECY

**The following questions and activation activity concede with Jacob's prophecy to the tribe of Issachar.**

*And of Zebulun he said, "Rejoice, Zebulun, in your going forth, And, Issachar, in your tents. They shall call peoples to the mountain; There they shall draw out the abundance of the seas, and the hidden treasures of the sand." (Deuteronomy 33:18)*

46. How did God make the distinction between Issachar and Zebulun?

47. Issachar, being the _____, knows of the _____ in the field and on the home front that are required of other soldiers and laborers.

48. Hype and charismatic thrills do not move a true Issachar. How do you recognize them? How have you responded to this in prophetic circles?

# ACTIVATION EXERCISE

Seek the Lord to plan an outreach where you met a practical need such as: feeding the homeless or helping a single mother or disadvantaged family. If possible, ask fellow Issachars and Zebuluns (whether they know their tribe or you have recognized their tribe) in the outreach. Ask the Lord a creative way to release prophetic words over the people you minister to. Follow up with these people after the outreach as well. Debrief together afterward about how the Lord used you together as a family unit regarding your tribal association. What unites you the most? How can you continue to unite as a tribe and with Zebuluns in ministry and fellowship?

49. Prophetically speaking, how do you feel the tribes of Issachar and Zebulun call people to the mountain of the Lord?

50. Issachar would be more of a _____ / _____ prophet, while Zebulun would be more of a _____ prophet.

51. What was the Father saying when He prophesied through Moses, *"they shall draw out the abundance of the seas, and the hidden treasures of the sand."*?

52. How have you been ensnared with the Martha syndrome, and why?

53. What is servanthood based on? What is it not based on?

54. Why is the tribe of Judah so pivotal to an Issachar struggling with the Martha syndrome?

55. How have lies of unworthiness kept you on a hamster wheel?

56. List five truths to destroy lies of unworthiness (and repeat them daily).

57. How can driving spirits and perfectionism cause an Issachar to become numb to his innate godly character?

58. How has your own stubbornness detoured your destiny?

59. How has stubbornness dulled your spiritual senses?

60. How was Elisha a poster child for his tribe? How do you identify with Elisha, and why?

# 12 Declarations for the Tribe of Issachar

1. I am ROYALTY! I bare the KING of GLORY wherever I go.

2. I am a STRONG WORKHORSE. Abba trusts me to carry the burdens of His heart and man's.

3. I am a WORTHY, UNASHAMED WORKMAN. I am diligent to carry out my Father's work His way!

4. I am a RESILIANT and NOBLE Bride. I am UNSTOPPABLE! I can do all things through Christ who strengthens me!

5. HUMILITY is my superpower! Bowing low is my love language.

6. I EMBRACE the Kingdom mandate with JOY! My heart and hands are never slothful.

7. EXCELLENCE and INTEGRITY are the core of my DNA.

8. I am a MAJESTIC DONKEY; I am a ROYAL SERVANT to the core.

9. I am the hands and feet of Yeshua. My ears and heart are tied to the cry of the poor.

10. I am a SINCERE and LOYAL servant whose humility arrests the heart of my Bridegroom!

11. When tied to PRAISE (Judah), I relinquish carrying Abba's workloads in striving like Martha and instead pour out my life to Him like Mary.

12. I choose to cease from striving and REST in my Beloved's sheepfolds. Under His shade I take great delight.

# Chapter 11

## Zebulun: The Haven for Souls

1. How has Yeshua been the haven for your soul?

2. What is the tribe of Zebulun called to be?

3. What will you find amongst the virtuous and endearing people of Zebulun?

4. What are some of the roles we find within the tribe of Zebulun?

5. How has Abba called Zebulun to seek out the chasms of the deep?

6. How does the Father bid you to go deep-sea diving in His nature?

7. What does the name of Zebulun mean?

8. Zebulun's Hebrew name is derived from which three Hebrew root words? How do you identify with each one?

## Journal Activity

Study and meditate on Luke 11:13 and Romans 3:23–25. What good gifts has the Father given you? How have these gifts given you an intimate revelation of who He is as Father? How do you celebrate these gifts? How can you share them with others?

9. Do a study on dowry in Scripture. What is the Lord revealing to you, and how does it apply to your relationship with Him?

10. Meditate on Genesis 3:7–11. How can you return to being clothed with the Father's nature as Adam and Eve were before the Fall?

11. What does being endowed with honor mean to you?

12. What code of honor has the Father revealed to you? How do you demonstrate this code of honor to the Lord, yourself, and others?

How does the Father call us to honor one another? Have a small group over for intimate fellowship and ministry time. Create several medals of honor (like worn in the military, a few for each person) prior to the meeting. Have everyone speak prophetically while pinning medals of honor on one another. Get creative and have fun!

13. The path of _____ brings us life, thereby possessing true _____ and holiness in Yeshua.

14. What does the Hebrew word *zibhe* mean?

15. The tribe of Zebulun forged a specific trade agreement with foreigners at Mount Tabor. What is the name of this trade agreement? What do you feel this speaks of prophetically?

16. If you are a Zebulun, has the Lord used you in marketplace ministry, or is He calling you to marketplace ministry?

17. What sacrifice(s) have you given wholeheartedly to the Lord that marked you in a profound way, and why?

18.

19. It is the workings of the _____ that brings us to the mountain of our _____.

20. The tribe of Zebulun, though valiant warriors, were known to be peacemakers. The Hebrew word for peace is *shalom*. The entomology for *shalom* meaning "the authority that destroys all chaos." How has Yeshua destroyed chaos in your life? How is He calling you to be a peacemaker?

## Journal Activity

The dwelling of one's soul is the essence of our matrimonial union with God Himself. In her book *Song of the Bride*, Jeanne Guyon speaks of the union of souls or dwelling in this way. Meditate on her quote mentioned on page 157 in *Living Stones* and journal.

21. What is the gemstone of Zebulun? What does it represent for Zebulun?

22. The symbol of Zebulun is a boat, particularly a sailboat. What prophetic treasures of Abba's nature does the sailboat hold for Zebulun?

23. Meditate on Hebrews 6:18–20. How has Yeshua been the anchor of your soul?

## JACOB'S PROPHECY

*Zebulun will dwell at the seashore; and he shall be a haven for ships, and his flank shall be toward Sidon.* (Genesis 49:13)

**The following questions and activity coincide with Jacob's prophecy to the tribe of Zebulun.**

24. What three things does the Father invite Zebulun to dwell upon?

25. How is Yeshua inviting you to *dwell at the seashore* with Him?

26. What promises has God given you that have brought you purpose on your journey with Him?

27. How have you placed self-imposed limits to God's promises?

**The Anchor Holds**: Make a creative board with an ocean theme. In your design make a large anchor representing Yeshua. Then make or find seashells and paint or draw each promise He has given you. Make daily declarations of God's faithfulness to you with each promise, and place them on the anchor for one week. Journal about what you gained from this exercise.

28. How has the Lord called you to be a haven for ships (souls)?

29. How can you serve the Lord as a minister of reconciliation?

30. How has compassion for souls been both a strength and a weakness for you? How does the Father want to bring balance to this beautiful gift within you?

31. Read and meditate on Isaiah 58:11–12. What is a true repairer of the breach? How can you repair the breach in the lives of those Abba has called you to minister to?

32. _____ is drawn from the healing nature of Yeshua.

33. How has the washing of the Word (Yeshua) restored the ancient ruins of your life?

34. How is the Lord calling you to bid others to His living water where they will find complete reconciliation, restoration, and revealing of God's heart and identity in Him?

35. What is the Lord speaking when Jacob prophesied, "His flank shall be toward Sidon"? What is the Lord speaking to your personally in this prophecy portion?

36. It is _____ that causes one to slumber, but _____ causes one to awaken to the _____ of God within.

# MOSES' PROPHECY

**The following questions and activity coincide with Moses' prophecy to the tribe of Zebulun.**

> *Of Zebulun he said, "Rejoice, Zebulun, in your going forth, and, Issachar, in your tents. They will call peoples to the mountain; There they will offer righteous sacrifices; for they will draw out the abundance of the seas, and the hidden treasures of the sand."*
> (Deuteronomy 33:18–19)

37. How is Zebulun uniquely marked with missions?

38. What differentiates Zebulun's ministry from the tribe of Issachar?

39. What giftings within Zebulun calls people to the mountain of the Lord?

# ACTIVATION EXERCISE

**Go Fish:** The tribe of Zebulun is known for being great fishers of men. In a time of prayer seek the Lord for a creative way to reach your community with the gospel. Gather others in this fishing expedition, and journal from your experience.

40. The tribe of Issachar is a pastoral/administrative prophet. What type of prophetic ministry and prophet is the tribe of Zebulun?

41. What treasures of wisdom have you discovered in your journey? How has the revelation of wisdom transformed you? How has the Lord called you to impart the treasures of wisdom to others?

42. Where have you been afraid to "rock the boat" and compromised? How has nonconfrontational behavior not only detoured your own destiny, but also the destiny of others?

43. Ask Holy Spirit how can you avoid the snare of the fear of man, and comment below.

44. When we don't _____ and _____ lie in the balance, we then have their blood on our hands.

45. How do you feel the Kingdom of God has suffered violence because of failure to confront the enemy? What is the true peacemaker's calling?

46. What havoc has toleration of control of others brought you? Are you ready to have a no-tolerance policy with the spirit of control?

47. What is the Lord's counsel and strategy for you to be free of control and the fear of man, while walking in your true identity as a peacemaker?

# Journal Activity

Judges 5:14 says, *"and out of Zebulun they that handle the pen of the writer."*

In a time of worship seek the Lord for revelation from the deep chasms of His word and nature. Scribe your revelations, and meditate on them. Repeat every day for a week. Journal from how this exercise caused you to grow in the gift of writing. Teach others from the revelation you receive.

# 12 Declarations For the Tribe of Zebulun

1. Yeshua is the HAVEN for my soul. I REST in His LOVE for me.

2. Yeshua is my Prince of PEACE. His SHALOM is the lighthouse that guides me HOME in the storms of life.

3. I am a PEACEMEAKER who radiates His PEACE.

4. Abba has called me to SEEK for the TREASURES of wisdom. I am a deep-sea diver of my Father's nature!

5. I am a HAVEN for storm-tossed souls. I bring RESTORATION where there has been devastation.

6. I am a PRICELESS GIFT of my Father. I am CLOTHED in the GLORY of my Father, which is my heavenly DOWRY.

7. I offer PURE and RIGHTEOUS sacrifices to my King, because He is WORTHY!

8. As I choose the fear of the Lord and SEEK for His WISDOM, treasures of the sand lie waiting for me to discover!

9. I am a FISHER of men. My heart beats for souls! I cast my nets and catch many fish for the Kingdom!

10. My flank is set toward Sidon. I have NO TOLERATION for the spirit of Jezebel!

11. The WAR COUNSELS Abba has entrusted me with bring lasting PEACE!

12. I set my sails with the WIND of the SPIRIT. Wherever the Father leads, I WILL GO!

# Chapter 12

## Manasseh: The Forgiving One

1. What is the cancelation of debt we could never pay?

2. Meditate on the following verse, and describe your intimate testimony of God's great love and forgiveness for you:

   *Instead of your* [former] *shame you shall have a twofold recompense; instead of dishonor and reproach* [your people] *shall rejoice in their portion. Therefore in their land they shall possess double* [what they had forfeited]; *everlasting joy shall be theirs.*
   (Isaiah 61:7 AMP)

3. If _____ by the precious _____ of Yeshua is the _____ of our soul, then forgiveness is our _____.

4. What does the Mercy Seat represent for us?

# ACTIVATION EXERCISE

Do a word study on the Hebrew words *kaporeth* and *kaphar*. How are you seated in Christ in heavenly places? How has the Father's mercy covered you? On a poster make one column with a heading of the Hebrew word *kaporeth* and a another column for *kaphar*. Under each column list at least five experiences where you have encountered the Father's mercy, using each of these two words' meaning.

5. What is the catalyst to enter into the holy place and the holy nature of God?

6. What two attributes of the Father have sealed your sonship in Him?

7. What is meaning of Manasseh's name?

8. How did the trials and triumphs of Manasseh's father Joseph form his own nature and tribe?

9. How do you identify with Joseph's story?

## Journal Activity

Ask the Holy Spirit where you have strived, or even presently are striving, for righteousness in your own strength and sought for justice by carnal means versus when you relied wholeheartedly on Abba's nature of forgiveness and mercy. What brought you breakthrough and restoration? How can you avoid snares of the former and live in the latter as a lifestyle?

19. Do you see yourself truly forgiven by God? If no, why? What lies are keeping you from receiving Abba's forgiveness for you?

20. Forgiveness is the pardon of _____, for it is for _____ that Christ has set us_____.

21. How does this tribe's gemstone serve as the Father's invitation to see the absence of your sin and not the presence of it?

22. Describe Manasseh's Kingdom role as a minister of transformation. How has the Lord called you to be a minister of transformation?

23. What does Joseph's Egyptian name, *Zaphnath-paaneah,* mean? What significance does it hold for you personally?

24. How does Manasseh's gemstone speak of character shaping? What has the Father used to mold His character within you?

The onyx also speaks to Manasseh's and Ephraim's gifts of prophetic dreaming and dream interpretation. Both tribes received this from their father, Joseph, who was known as a "possessor of dreams." How has He called you to be a possessor of dreams? Ask the Father to reveal the mysteries of His heart. Seek to "dream His dreams." Record and journal them for one month.

***Optional Creative Activity:** Using these dreams as inspiration, make a redemption dream board.

25. How can the gift of dreams, revelation, and seeing become tainted with spiritual mixing? Have you personally experienced or witnessed this? What is the key to purity in these gifts and callings for Manasseh?

26. How have you experienced the dark night of the soul? How did the Lord bring you out of this season? What transformation occurred within you from out of the dark night of the soul season?

27. Manasseh is called to recount the _____ of God and the relinquishment of _____ and condemnation's _____.

28. What is Manasseh's God-given character of mercy formed in?

29. The symbol of Manasseh is the palm tree. What connotations does the palm tree hold for the tribe of Manasseh?

30. As a royal palm tree, how can you plant your roots deep in the heart and nature of God?

31. A palm tree endures many elements of the atmosphere around it: rain, wind, and heat. How have you endured these elements and been transformed as an upright palm tree in Abba's Kingdom?

    A. Rain:

    B. Wind:

    C. Heat:

32. How has the fruit of long-suffering been cultivated in your life? Where are you lacking the fruit of long-suffering?

33. The nature of longsuffering is a _____ of Heaven's _____. It never _____, but bears and champions _____.

34. Manasseh goes through often long periods of refinement on the back side of the desert. Describe your desert season and the refinement that took place during that time.

35. Forgiveness comes solely through the incorruptible _____ of Yeshua. There is no stability outside of the work of the _____.

# ACTIVATION EXERCISE

Meditate on Isaiah 64:1, Psalm 68:9, and II Chronicles 6:26–28. These scriptures reveal the mercy cry the tribe of Manasseh is called to release in the earth. In a time of prayer seek the Lord how to release the mercy cry that is within you with a prophetic act.

36. Manasseh has the innate ability to be sustained by grace during extreme seasons of testing and blessing. How has this been true in your journey with the Lord?

37. How do you feel the seven years of plenty and then seven years of famine formed the character (and his tribe) of young Manasseh? What legacy did Joseph leave for his sons that was a catalyst to their destinies? How does this speak to you today?

# JACOB'S PROPHECY

*"Joseph is a fruitful bough, A fruitful bough by a spring; Its branches run over a wall. The archers bitterly attacked him, and shot at him and harassed him; But his bow remained firm, And his arms were agile, from the hands of the Mighty One of Jacob (From there is the Shepherd, the Stone of Israel), from the God of your father who helps you, And by the Almighty who blesses you with blessings of heaven above, Blessings of the deep that lies beneath, Blessings of the breasts and of the womb. The blessings of your father have surpassed the blessings of my ancestors up to the utmost bound of the everlasting hills; may they be on the head of Joseph, and on the crown of the head of the one distinguished among his brothers."* (Genesis 49:22–26)

**The following questions and activity coincide with Jacob's prophecy to the tribe of Manasseh.**

38. How did Joseph embody the fruitful bough as his father Jacob prophesied? What spiritual DNA markers did this leave for Manasseh and Ephraim and their tribes?

39. How does Manasseh learn to walk in true abiding?

40. "Fruitful bough" stems from what Hebrew word? What is its prophetic meaning?

41. Explain the "law of return." What is its significant connection for the tribes of Manasseh and Ephraim?

42. How does Manasseh prophetically exemplify a fruitful bough by the spring? What relation does this have to Manasseh's mercy call?

Manasseh: The Forgiving One

43. What can endanger Manasseh to die on the vine?

44. The following portion of Jacob's prophecy refers specifically to Joseph's dark night of the soul season. This also formed the character of Manasseh and Ephraim and their tribes.

    "*The archers bitterly attacked him, and shot at him and harassed him; But his bow remained firm, and his arms were agile . . .*"

    How has persecution served as the anvil of transformation in your own life?

45. _____ is an _____ of the nature of Christ and the work of the _____ within us.

46. Corrie Ten Boom stated, "When we confess ours sins . . . God casts them into the deepest ocean, gone forever . . . I believe God places a sign out there that says, NO FISHING ALLOWED."[i]

    What experiences in life has God posted His NO FISHING ALLOWED sign while doing a deep-rooted work of forgiveness in you?

47. According to this portion of the prophecy, "*From there is the Shepherd, the Stone of Israel . . . .*" What type of leadership roles do Manasseh and Ephraim hold in the Kingdom?

48. How is Manasseh uniquely different from his brother tribe Ephraim in how they express their gifts and callings?

173

49. How did the Father make a distinction with Joseph's sons and the other tribes? What do you feel is the prophetic significance of this distinction?

50. Read Genesis 47:8–22. What is the depth of what the Father is speaking through Manasseh's and Ephraim's entrance into the family when Jacob blessed them in this scripture passage?

# Journal Activity

Take a time of deep contemplation of the prophetic significance of the right and left hand of God and what this means for Manasseh and Ephraim. Do you feel a stronger emphasis of the left hand or the right hand of God in your own walk with Him? Is your revelation of one hand experientially atrophied in a distorted personal perception? How does the Lord want to bring you balance so that both the right and left hand of God are equal in your life?

# MOSES' PROPHECY

*Of Joseph he said, "Blessed of the Lord be his land, with the choice things of heaven, with the dew, And from the deep lying beneath, And with the choice yield of the sun, And with the choice produce of the months. And with the best things of the ancient mountains, And with the choice things of the everlasting hills, And with the choice things of the earth and its fullness, and the favor of Him who dwelt in the bush. Let it come to the head of Joseph, and to the crown of the head of the one distinguished among his brothers. As the firstborn of his ox, majesty is his and his horns are the horns of the wild ox; with them he will push the peoples, All at once, to the ends of the earth, and those are the ten thousands of Ephraim, And those are the thousands of Manasseh."*
(Deuteronomy 33:13–17)

**The following questions and activity coincide with Moses' prophecy to the tribe of Manasseh.**

51. How has the Lord blessed the land of Joseph through the tribes of Manasseh and Ephraim? Do an in-depth study on past and present development of their lands. Specifically look into the region of Jericho (Ephraim) and Manasseh (Megiddo). Is there disrepair in the present? How do you feel the Father longs to bring total restoration to current day Israel in Manasseh's and Ephraim's territories?

ACTIVATION EXERCISE

In a time of prayer, ask the Father for the mercy cry for the territories and inheritance of Manasseh and Ephraim. Hold and intercession watch using the specific mercy call He gives you and others.

Manasseh: The Forgiving One

10. What is the road to forgiveness paved with for the tribe of Manasseh?

11. What has the Father marked the tribe of Manasseh within the work of the ministry and their lives?

12. How has past suffering, persecution, and false accusation brought trauma in your life? How have you been restored by the Father in these areas of your life? What areas do you still need restoration in?

13. Read and meditate on II Corinthians 1:4–6. How have you found abundance in Christ's sufferings in your life? How have you found the abundance of His comfort?

14. _____ is a foundational part of the Father's _____.

15. What is Manasseh instinctively in tune with, and why?

16. What are vital Kingdom keys to release chains of bondage and restore the ancient ruins of our lives?

17. What gemstone does Manasseh share with his brother Ephraim?

18. How does Manasseh's gemstone speak of Abba's forgiveness?

52. Both Manasseh and Ephraim can lay hold of the significance of the ox as a prophetic symbol. What does it specifically represent for the tribe of Manasseh?

53. How is Manasseh called to "push the peoples" alongside Ephraim in the end times?

54. How is the tribe of Manasseh extremely significant even though their numbers are far fewer than that of Ephraim? What is the Father's wisdom in this?

55. Study the life of Gideon in Judges chapters 6–8. How is Gideon the poster child for the tribe of Manasseh?

56. How did Gideon successfully confront idolatry in Israel? How did Gideon waver? How do you personally identify with Gideon if you are a Manasseh?

57. What is the purpose of Kingdom covert ops? Why is the tribe of Manasseh especially called to be the covert-op tribe? What Kingdom covert ops has the Lord enlisted you for in His end-time army?

58. How does Manasseh come into their dominion by being an oasis in the earth?

59. Read Joshua 17:1–6. As a Manasseh, how can you fearlessly possess your inheritance like the daughters of Zelophehad?

60. What prophetic significance and end-time purpose does Megiddo hold for the tribe of Manasseh and their role?

# 12 Declarations For the Tribe of Manasseh

1. Because Abba's LOVE and MERCY has been lavishly and freely given to me, I can FORGIVE and FORGET my sin, shame, condemnation, and trauma of the past.

2. God will ADD His GOODNESS to me as I ABIDE in Yeshua.

3. Like my tribe's stone, the onyx, I am black but LOVELY!

4. I am seated with Christ in heavenly places upon His Mercy Seat. His MERCY is my COVERING and gives me access to Abba's GLORY!

5. I am a ROYAL palm tree who stands UPRIGHT in the house of my Father!

6. I bend FREELY with the wind of the Spirit. Winds of chaos will NO LONGER move or uproot me!

7. I am SUPERNATURALLY acclimated to the spiritual atmosphere.

8. I am called to resound the MERCY CALL in the earth.

9. I am a FRUITFUL BOUGH by the springs of Living Water flowing from Abba's throne!

10. Abba has FAVORED me with His LEFT HAND. I carry the mercy call to the earth!

11. Abba has designed me to be a REPAIRER of the breach, a minister of His TRANSFORMATION GLORY!

12. Like the daughters of Zelophehad, I will FEARLESSLY POSSESS my inheritance!

---

[i] Corrie Ten Boom, *Tramp For The Lord* (Fort Washington, Pennsylvania; Christian Literature Crusade, Old Tappan, New Jersey: Fleming H. Revell Company 1974) Page 55.

# Chapter 13

## Ephraim: The Fruitful Vine

1. How can you truly put on the mind of Christ?

2. What do feel the abundant life in Christ is that John 10:10 speaks of?

3. Abiding calls us to surrender the _____ in order to abide in the will and nature of the Father.

4. Read and meditate on Colossians 1:18–20. How does the fullness dwell in Christ?

5. How can we enter into that fullness?

6. What does Ephraim's name mean?

7. How was Ephraim and Manasseh's birth(s) profoundly prophetic?

8. The Father's supply is _____ because His nature is _____.

9. Do a Hebrew word study on the Father's Hebrew name YHVH Yireh (Jehovah Jireh). How has He revealed Himself to you as YHVH Yireh (Jehovah Jireh)?

10. As a watchman, what motivates an Ephraimite?

11. What should the tribe of Ephraim be as an administer in the Kingdom? What should they be careful not to do?

12. Ephraim shares the onyx with the tribe of Manasseh. Describe the prophetic meaning of the redemptive facet for the tribe of Ephraim.

13. What spiritual gift does Ephraim share with the tribe of Levi? How is this gift uniquely different to Levi's?

14. How do we see Ephraim's gift of apostolic administration in the onyx?

15. The onyx also speaks of this tribe's gifting as a seer. The prophet Samuel was a known seer/prophet who hailed from Ephraim. What do you see Samuel mirroring for Ephraim in I Samuel 9:15–19?

16. What are two tribal symbols that speak of Abba's nature within the tribe of Ephraim? Which one is Ephraim's captain tribe symbol?

17. Define the Hebrew word *chazaq*. What is the significance of this word in context of Numbers 13:17–33 and the tribe of Ephraim?

# Living Stones Study Guide

18. What is the prophetic significance of the valley of Eschol? What does this revelation speak to you of God's heart for you?

19. What key fruit is needed to gain our inheritance?

20. Ephraimites are ministers of _____ who call the Body to _____ in the fruit of _____.

21. Ephraimites learn the ministry of _____ by first becoming _____.

22. How does the fruitful vine speak of Ephraim's calling to discipleship in relation to abiding in Yeshua?

23. What does Ephraim's gift of multiplication speak of? How does this gift serve the Body of Messiah?

24. What are oxen synonymous of in the Bible?

## Journal Activity

Meditating on Isaiah 53:2–12, dive into the revelation where Yeshua is depicted as the Suffering Servant. What depth of the Father's love do you see in this prophecy about Him? If you are an Ephraimite, how is the Lord inviting you to share in His nature portrayed in Isaiah 53:2–12?

25. Ephraim's call to servanthood calls them to do what daily?

# ACTIVATION EXERCISE

**The "I" Factor**: Find a two-sided mirror, with one side clearly visible and the other side magnifying. (Two separate mirrors will also work as long as one is distorted or proportions exaggerated.) Taking the magnified (or distorted) mirror, write a big capital letter "I" on the mirror to represent the old self and facades. In a time of deep heart-seeking, look intently into the "I" distorted mirror side. Ask the Lord to gently reveal where you have allowed the old self, or the "I" factor, to keep you bound in facades. Write what is revealed down to you and renounce these "I" factor distortions in a Spirit-led time of repentance. Now look intently a second time into the mirror, this time gazing into the clear undistorted mirror and make seven declarations of who you are in Christ. Journal about this experience.

26. How is the Lord calling you to be like the Samaritan and stop for the one? Ask the Lord how you can implement servanthood in your daily life.

27. Meditate on the following scripture:

*Where there are no oxen, the manger is empty, but from the strength of an ox comes an abundant harvest.* (Proverbs 14:4 NIV)

How can Ephraim as an ox gain strengh from abding? How does this relate propehtically to the harvest and souls in Ephriam's life and ministry?

28. How has your own self-sufficiency called you out of abiding in the Vine?

## Jacob's Prophecy

*"Joseph is a fruitful bough, A fruitful bough by a spring; Its branches run over a wall. The archers bitterly attacked him, and shot at him and harassed him; But his bow remained firm, And his arms were agile, from the hands of the Mighty One of Jacob (From there is the Shepherd, the Stone of Israel), from the God of your father who helps you, And by the Almighty who blesses you with blessings of heaven above, Blessings of the deep that lies beneath, Blessings of the breasts and of the womb. The blessings of your father have surpassed the blessings of my ancestors up to the utmost bound of the everlasting hills; may they be on the head of Joseph, and on the crown of the head of the one distinguished among his brothers"* (Genesis 49:22-26).

**The following questions coincide with Jacob's prophecy to the tribe of Ephraim.**

29. How is Ephraim a fruitful bough by a spring?

30. How can abiding sustain Ephraim in times of persecution?

31. How can we remain fruitful during the dark night of the soul?

32. How does Ephraim personify this portion of the prophecy in light of their tribe embodying the right hand of God? How does this relate to the glory of God and the end-time move of God?

> *And by the Almighty who blesses you with blessings of heaven above, Blessings of the deep that lies beneath, Blessings of the breasts and of the womb. The blessings of your father have surpassed the blessings of my ancestors up to the utmost bound of the everlasting hills . . .*

33. How does abiding bring the tribe Ephraim favor like their forefather Joseph, who crowned as Israel prophesied, *"on the crown of the head of the one distinguished among his brothers"*?

## MOSES' PROPHECY

> *Of Joseph he said, "Blessed of the Lord be his land, with the choice things of heaven, with the dew, And from the deep lying beneath, And with the choice yield of the sun, And with the choice produce of the months. And with the best things of the ancient mountains, And with the choice things of the everlasting hills, And with the choice things of the earth and its fullness, and the favor of Him who dwelt in the bush. Let it come to the head of Joseph, and to the crown of the head of the one distinguished among his brothers. As the firstborn of his ox, majesty is his and his horns are the horns of the wild ox; with them he will push the peoples, All at once, to the ends of the earth, and those are the ten thousands of Ephraim, And those are the thousands of Manasseh."*
> *(Deuteronomy 33:13–17)*

## Ephraim: The Fruitful Vine

**The following questions and activity coincide with Moses' prophecy to the tribe of Ephraim.**

34. How has the Lord blessed the land of Joseph through the tribes of Manasseh and Ephraim? Do an in-depth study on past and present development of their lands. Specifically look into the region of Jericho (Ephraim) and Manasseh (Megiddo). Is there disrepair in the present? How do you feel the Father longs to bring total restoration to current-day Israel in Manasseh's and Ephraim's territories?

35. _____ is the nature of God to _____ the abundance of Himself and His Kingdom.

## ACTIVATION EXERCISE

Research the life and ministry of Rees Howells in his biography by Norman Grubb called *Intercessor*. What lessons can you learn from Rees's life in abiding and intercession? Ask the Father how you can come into a place of abiding for the fullness of His glory to be restored into the earth. Journal from your experience.

36. How is Ephraim called to "push the peoples" alongside Manasseh in the end times?

37. To abide is to _____ from the spirit of the _____ and abide in the Spirit of _____.

38. Ephraimites have adventurous spirits that can turn into licentiousness. When this stronghold is unchecked, it can cause them to lose sight of what?

39. Study I Corinthians 10:20–22. Describe true communion with the Lord and drinking from His cup versus when we entertain the spirit of the world and drink of the cup of demons. How has the spirit of the world enticed you? How did the Lord call you into freedom?

40. When does Satan have a legal right with a believer?

41. What does abiding in Christ require of us?

42. If the tribe of Ephraim possesses fullness of their identity by abiding in fruitfulness or multiplication, what naturally opposes them?

## ACTIVATION EXERCISE

**Catch the Foxes**: Make a creative board with a vineyard and grapes. Have your gifts, callings, strengths, dreams, and victories labeled on clusters of grapes. Then design little fox cutouts and label them as the weaknesses and lies of the enemy that are stealing from your vines. As each fox is put up, take down the fruit it devours from you. Then as a prophetic act, renounce each fox and replace corresponding fruit back in its proper place in your vineyard. Now celebrate what you've cultivated with the Lord!

43. How did generational idolatry enter into Ephraim's family line and later cause division? How has this happened in your own life?

44. Study I Kings 11:26–40. How did Jeroboam's idolatry breed chaos in the spiritual atmosphere in Israel? How has this still affected Israel today? What is God's heart and plan of restoration for His Kingdom?

45. Define the façade of envy and the role it has had in detouring the tribe of Ephraim. Have you struggled with envy? How has it detoured your destiny?

46. Meditate on the love story in Hosea 13:1–16. How have you been like Gomer in your life? How did the Lord restore your first love with Him?

47. Studying the lives of Joshua and Samuel, how did they learn abiding and cultivate a fruitful life of intimacy with the Lord? What foxes detoured them? What strengths served as a catalyst to not only their own destinies, but for Israel's destiny also?

48. As a daughter of Ephraim, how did Hannah abide for the double portion the Lord favored her with? How is the Lord calling you to do the same?

49. Study Ezekiel 37:20–22. Seeking the Lord wholeheartedly, how can you participate in this final end-time move of God?

# 12 Declarations for the Tribe of Ephraim

1. I am a FRUITFUL VINE who ABIDES in Yeshua, the lover of my soul.

2. I CULTIVATE fruitfulness through INTIMACY with my Beloved.

3. I am a FRUIT PRODUCER in my Father's Kingdom. He alone will ADD and MULTIPLY my destiny!

4. God has made me FRUITFUL in the land of affliction.

5. I CATCH the little foxes that spoil my vines. I bear the fruit of REPENTANCE.

6. In my onyx stone, I carry the REDEMPTIVE facet for souls. I am a minister of RECONCILIATION.

7. I drink from the CUP OF THE LORD. I renounce the cup of demons, and the spirit of the world will not entice me anymore!

8. As I ABIDE in the VISION of the Lord, I am made BOLD and COURAGEOUS!

9. The STOREHOUSES of Heaven are waiting for me to faithfully ADMINISTRATE abundance to my Father's Kingdom.

10. I am a WATCHMEN who ABIDES in the nature of Christ and intercedes from the mind of Christ, doing the will of my Father.

11. I am a STRONG OX who pushes others into their destiny. I am a selfless servant, carrying the burden of Christ and of my brethren.

12. I am CROSSING OVER into the land of my inheritance, The FULLNESS of CHRIST is my glorious INHERITANCE!

# Chapter 14

# Benjamin: The Beloved

1. Meditating on Matthew 18:1–4, how can you come to Abba as a dependent child, full of childlike wonder?

2. Salvation affords us not only the entrance into the Kingdom of Heaven, but it is the continual process of making *aliyah* (to ascend or return) to the Father. How do we make aliyah as the sons of God?

3. What instinctual awareness does the tribe of Benjamin possess?

4. Describe the progression of maturity of the Shulamite's love for her Bridegroom in the Song of Songs. Symbolically speaking, where are you personally on your journey in Song of Songs?

5. The events surrounding Benjamin's birth have a profound significance on his life and on his tribe. Prior to Benjamin's birth, his father, Jacob, had an encounter with the Lord. Read Genesis 32:24–28. How did this have a profound significance for the tribe of Benjamin?

Benjamin: The Beloved

6. What beautiful mystery is found for Benjamin and the Body in Genesis 35:19?

7. What is Benjamin's name in Hebrew? What does it mean prophetically?

8. What is Benjamin's calling as a seal upon the family of God? By nature and calling, what has God appointed the tribe of Benjamin to do?

9. Describe the war to birth Benjamin and its prophetic significance. Has the Lord called you to birth something tremendous in the Kingdom? Have you experienced incredible warfare where the enemy tried to abort it?

10. Upon birthing Benjamin, Rachel was hemorrhaging to death when she named him what instead? What is the deep prophetic meaning behind this name, and who does it reveal?

11. _____ knows when radical _____, _____ makers, and fearless _____ are about to be birthed.

# Journal Activity

Benjamin's father, Israel, came into his identity and dominion just prior to his birth. The nation of Israel itself has had to wrestle for its identity and dominion. How do you see a travail in Heaven for the Jewish people to come into their identity and destiny? What is the Father calling you to do see Jewish people come into this glorious destiny?

12. Regarding sonship, describe what Abba was prophetically birthing in the Kingdom through Reuben, and what has it consummated in Benjamin?

13. Benjamin's particular stone is the green jasper (a deep green/blue color) with splatters or striations of red. What deep significance do the red striations on the jasper hold for the tribe of Benjamin?

14. How does the jasper stone speak of a decree of adoption for Benjamin?

15. Read Romans 8:14–19. The jasper stone has the ability to transform from its blue green state to a clear jasper stone. What does this speak of prophetically to you personally in light of this scripture?

# Jacob's Prophecy

*"Benjamin is a ravenous wolf; In the morning he devours the prey, and in the evening he divides the spoil."* (Genesis 49:27)

**The following questions and activity coincide with Jacob's prophecy to the tribe of Benjamin.**

16. Define the terms *ravenous* and *ravenous appetite*.

17. What was Yeshua speaking of in Matthew 6:24? How does this reflect Jacob's prophecy when he says, *"Benjamin is a ravenous wolf..."*?

18. How have you feasted on mammon in your own life? How did the Lord free you and give you a holy hunger?

19. What can make our appetites holy or profane?

20. What life lesson of his own caused Jacob to prophesy this word of warning and correction to Benjamin? How can you learn from Jacob's insight and warning?

21. Define the Hebrew word *nephesh*.

22. Define the Hebrew word *akal*.

23. Read Judges 19:17–30. How did the tribe of Benjamin allow their spiritual appetites to become profaned? How did this cause them to spiral into grave deception and sin?

24. What are the sons of Belial? How did the other tribes try to restore the tribe of Benjamin after this incident? What did this incident cost the tribe of Benjamin?

25. How does Jacob's prophecy, "in the morning he devours the prey," speak of Benjamin's immaturity?

26. What spiritual abuses in the Body of Messiah do you see as truly ravenous and guile in nature? How does the Lord want to bring freedom and restoration to His Bride?

27. Benjamin is known as the son of God's right hand therefore he possesses it. How does Benjamin likewise possess the left hand of God? How does this speak of the dominion that Benjamin is mandated to carry?

28. What portion of Jacob's prophecy to Benjamin speaks of his tribe coming into maturity?

29. What occurs during the "lone wolf" stage of Benjamin's journey? How has the Lord led you into a season of separation where you experienced great refinement and accelerated growth?

30. Why is dominion a journey and not automatic?

31. What does a Benjamin begin his/her lone wolf stage with?

## ACTIVATION EXERCISE

**You Are What You Eat:** In a time of deep soul searching, come before the Father and ask Him what you have truly been feasting on spiritually. What has your nepsh (soul) been dining on? As a prophetic act, ask Holy Spirit to reveal foods in the natural that reflect what the Father revealed to you. Prepare these foods and partake of them for whatever amount of time the Holy Spirit asks of you to illustrate a valuable lesson. Now go back to the Father and ask Him how to daily feast on His will for you. Then ask the Holy Spirit what healthy, nourishing foods represent the Father's will and feast upon it, however the Holy Spirit gives you freedom to do so.

32. Read Matthew 4:1–4. How did Yeshua feast on the Father's will and defy the soulish appetite?

33. What occurs when the lone wolf seeks for the shelter of the Lord?

34. How does a Benjamin find protection from his predator?

35. What does it mean for a Benjamin to find his mate and join his pack? Have you come to this place in your journey with the Lord?

## MOSES' PROPHECY

*Of Benjamin he said, "May the beloved of the Lord dwell in security by Him, who shields him all the day, and he dwells between His shoulders." (Deuteronomy 33:12)*

**The following questions and activity coincide with Moses' prophecy to the tribe of Benjamin.**

36. What knowledge does a true Benjaminite rest in?

37. A true Benjaminite knows how to possess a _____ rooted in true _____ _____.

38. How is the Father calling you to walk in childlike abandon?

39. How do Benjaminites possess uninhibited faith?

40. How does Benjamin rest between Yeshua's shoulders? Prophetically speaking, what rests upon Yeshua's shoulders in Scripture?

41. How has the orphan spirit separated you from the love and image of Abba Father?

42. When a Benjamin cannot see that he is made in the likeness of God as *Benyamin, son of my right hand*, what does he become enslaved to?

43. Below are the characteristics of the orphan spirit. Define each characteristic and how you have struggled with it. Which ones have you overcome, and how did you find freedom?

    *Abandonment:*

    *Shame:*

    *Doubt:*

*Alienation:*

*Hopelessness:*

*Stigma through speculation:*

*Poverty:*

Make a royal decree of adoption. Use as many references to your spiritual DNA/identity according to your tribe as possible. Ask Abba for His declarations regarding who you are made to be according to His likeness (glory nature) in you. Boldly proclaim your decree of adoption every day for one week. Journal from your experience.

44. What are the two ways poverty can come and rob the believer?

45. How did the circumstances surrounding Benjamin's birth oppose his God-given dominion and make him prey to the facades of the orphan spirit and poverty?

46. What did Yeshua have to say about ministering to the poor? Study His ministry to the poor and how the early Church cared for each other. Also, study scriptures where God rebukes those who oppress the poor. How can we have humility and unconditional love toward others and ourselves in this often polarizing subject of the poor and poverty? How does Abba want you to bring reformation and healing in this area?

47. Read Genesis 42:15–38 and Genesis 44:10–12. Joseph summoned his brother Benjamin to test him. How was the Lord bringing young Benjamin to task regarding his soul? How did Benjamin bring restoration to Joseph and his brothers?

## Journal Activity

Do an in-depth word study on the reversal of fortune in Scripture. Ask the Lord to give you an application for your daily life. In your quiet time, ask Abba what areas He is longing to bring a reversal of fortune in your life. How does the Father want to bring you into the fullness of your destiny? How is He restoring your inheritance?

48. Read I Samuel 8:4–22. How was King Saul's spiritual appetite indicative of the nation of Israel prior to (and during) his reign?

49. How does the story of King Saul's life serve as a cautionary tale to the tribe of Benjamin?

50. How did Saul engage in the lies of the orphan spirit? What snowball effect did this have, leading to his demise?

51. How did King Saul allow the leaven of rebellion to grow in his life and become the sin of witchcraft?

52. How has rebellion detoured you from your destiny? How has the Father brought alignment that restored you on the right path?

53. _____ is like a _____ _____ to the door of our heart that tells Satan, "Come on in and make yourself at home."

54. What does the idol of self have roots in?

55. When the idol of self is ruling us, what are we denying in the Kingdom?

56. What was the jasper transformation of the Apostle Paul? How was Paul a true Benjaminite? How did his transformation build a legacy for the gospel?

57. The following Benjaminites were great selfless deliverers and heroes in Scripture and history. Briefly tell of how each one made a profound impact in the Kingdom. What spiritual DNA markers of the tribe of Benjamin do you see in each one? What facades did they overcome? How do you identify with them personally?

    A. Jonathan:

    B. Abner:

    C. Saint Francis of Assisi:

    D. Mordecai:

    E. Queen Esther:

# 12 Declarations
## For the Tribe of Benjamin

1. I am a BLISSFUL, CHILDLIKE Bride of Yeshua, full of Abba's wonder and dancing in His Fields of GRACE!

2. I am NO ORPHAN! I am a SON OF GOD!

3. Abba and all of Heaven CELEBRATES me; I am His FAVORITE ONE! Unmerited favor is part of my inheritance in Christ.

4. I possess TENACIOUS FAITH! I am SECURE in Abba's nature and do mighty exploits for His Kingdom!

5. My SONSHIP is the seal of my IDENTITY. I am a SON of His RIGHT HAND and walk in Kingdom DOMINION!

6. I am the BELOVED of the LORD, and His DESIRE is toward me!

7. I carry a POWERFUL breaker anointing and special FAVOR from the Lord! I am SPIRITUAL DYNAMITE! *BOOM!*

8. My infectious CHILDLIKE faith and love is a CATALYST that builds Abba's Kingdom!

9. I am a ravenous lover of God and His Word. I am consumed with HOLY HUNGER. My meat and drink is to do the WILL of my Father.

10. I ANNIHILATE the orphan spirit as I am SECURE in Abba's LOVE and my IDENTITY. I break chains of poverty, shame, stigmas, and rejection wherever I go!

11. As I daily SURRENDER my will, I walk in RADICAL DOMINION that shifts Heaven and earth!

12. Like Queen Esther, Yeshua has extended His scepter to me and given me the FULLNESS of His Kingdom. I receive His REVERSAL of FORTUNE for me and use it to bring restoration to Abba's family!

# Chapter 15

# The New Jerusalem:

## THE HABITATION OF THE LIVING GOD

1. In the process of your journey of coming into habitation and thereby discovering your identity in Christ in the one of the twelve tribes, what have you learned the most? How have you transformed?

2. What reveals identity?

3. How have you encountered the Father face to face? How can you live the unveiled life as His image bearer?

4. What is our ultimate destiny to discover?

5. What facades have distorted the image of the Father that you are destined to mirror? How have you gained victory over these facades?

6. In what tribe did you truly discover your identity and blossom in your intimacy with Abba and Yeshua as you read *Living Stones*?

7. How have you encountered the glory of God revealing who you are as a son of God to your core? What mistaken identity did the glory strip away?

8. How has Yeshua pursued you and revealed your identity as His Bride? What is the story of your heavenly courtship with Him?

9. How do you see yourself in the "Bride Made Ready" story? Can you feel the intense love of the Bridegroom toward you

10. Reading the two encounters in the New Jerusalem, what pulls on your heartstrings the most? How do you see yourself in the New Jerusalem?

11. Define *maon kadosh*.

12. How do we possess *maon kadosh* with Abba and Yeshua?

13. Study and meditate on Isaiah 66. How does this Messianic prophecy reveal the great mystery of habitation?

14. What does Isaiah 66 reveal for Israel? What is the Gentiles' role in serving the Lord and the Jewish people in this scripture?

15. How do you see the true Bride revealed in Isaiah 66 versus the apostate Church? How do you relate to this juxtaposition personally?

16. According to Isaiah 66, what roles do some Gentiles have alongside the Jewish people?

## Journal Activity

Take a more in-depth look at Isaiah 66. Study and meditate on it, immersing yourself in the glory of the Kingdom Age of Messiah's return and reign. During a time of worship, see yourself as an integral part of the Kingdom Age. Journal about this experience and study.

17. The _____ do not stop operating in the New Jerusalem, but rather they reach their _____.

18. Why will there be schools of worship, the prophetic, and other areas of ministry in the New Jerusalem if salvation has reached its fullness in the Kingdom?

19. What do we look forward to entering into in the New Jerusalem?

20. Explain how we reach the fullness of being the family of God in the New Jerusalem. How does this specifically relate to each tribe?

21. Who is the Melchizedek, and what is His role in the New Jerusalem?

22. What role do the Feasts of the Lord play in the New Jerusalem?

23. What is the Millennial Reign of Christ, ultimately?

24. Meditate on the following verse:

    *He chooses our inheritance for us, the glory of Jacob whom He loves. Selah.* (Psalm 47:4)

    How do feel the Lord has uniquely chosen you, and how have you found your inheritance as a son/daughter of Jacob?

25. How does God's promise to Abraham in Genesis 22:17 reach fulfillment? How does this tie in with Hebrews 11 where Abraham is mentioned and this promise?

26. Study and meditate on Ezekiel chapters 40–48. What do they reveal of the Kingdom Age and Messianic Reign?

27. What mystery does Ezekiel 48 reveal?

28. What is the Spirit Flood? What is the tole of the Spirit in the New Jerusalem?

29. How does the Spirit Flood relate to the prophetic promise in Habakkuk 2:14? How does this relate to the revealing of the sons of God mentioned in Romans 8?

30. The Holy Spirit is the _____ of _____.

31. What is the correlation between Ezekiel's Temple and the one mentioned in Revelation 21? What mystery is revealed here?

32. What do the "heads" speak of in Psalm 24:7?

33. List and describe which tribes are found at each set of directional gates and their roles in the Millennial Kingdom. Take your time and go deep into this revelation. Comment on the one you find yourself in (your own tribe). What role(s) is the Lord revealing to you in which you will be partaking of in the Millennial Reign? Each set of gates has three tribes (one has four when counting Manasseh and Ephraim separately).

The North Gates:

The South Gates:

The East Gates:



The West Gates:

## ACTIVATION EXERCISE

In a time of prayer, seek the Lord on how to host a Kingdom Gate Party (kind of like the idea of a Block Party, but using the tribes and their respective gates in the New Jerusalem). Learning what you have on the twelve tribes of Israel, and knowing your spiritual family and friends that you fellowship with, ask Holy Spirit how to creatively activate each one in an intimate night of worship, prophetic ministry, and fellowship. Journal about this experience, and process with those who attend.

34. What will you never find in the Kingdom?

35. What will the Millennial Reign of Christ be?

36. What roles do Abba and Yeshua have in the Temple during the Millennial Reign?

# ACTIVATION EXERCISE

Contemplate on Revelation 21 and the tribes with their stones listed on pages 236–237 of *Living Stones*. How has the Church reached her glorious destiny in each one? Describe each one below and their stone. Make a decree of identity for each tribe. How has each become a brilliant living stone reflecting the Head, which is Yeshua?

(1) Benjamin:

(2) Dan:

(3) Levi:

(4) Judah:

(5) Joseph or Manasseh and Ephraim:


(6) Reuben:


(7) Zebulun:


(8) Naphtali:


(9) Simeon:

(10) Asher:

(11) Gad:

(12) Issachar:

37. What is the prophetic meaning of the man-child mentioned in Revelation 12:5?

## Journal Activity

Reflecting on the wealth Abba has given us in the revelation of the twelve tribes, who are you as His living stone? How would you define worth differently than when you began? How has your perception changed of how the Father sees you and how you see yourself?

***Optional Creative Activity: Make a royal decree of sonship and design a ketubah (wedding contract) between you and Yeshua. Host a night of intimate worship including a vow ceremony to the Lord as His Bride, with a time of communion and prophetic ministry.

# LIVING STONES STUDY GUIDE

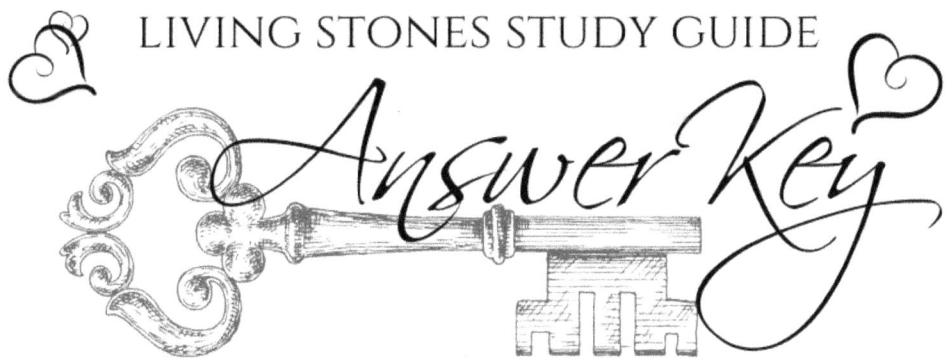

This Answer Key coincides with the relating chapter in both the Study Guide and the *Living Stones* book. Questions regarding your own personal answers, journal and acitvation excercises are not listed within this Answer Key. Under no circumstances should answers be graded. This book serves as a study tool and for the sole purpose inward growth and transformation.

## Introduction

5. maon
17. who, destiny
23. breastplate, wilderness camping/marching order, New Jerusalem
24. lion, ox, man eagle
25. 1) Judah the lion, 2) Reuben the man, 3) Ephraim the ox, 4) Dan the eagle

## Chapter 1:
### Your journey into habitation with the Living God

1. Hebrew for "returning or ascending"
3. the orphan spirit
5. graces
9. slaves, free, communion, truth, Kingdom
10. A façade is a false perception, lie, or appearance opposing the heart of God.
12. accusation, unity, communion, Kingdom
14. truth

# Chapter 2

## Reuben: The Passionate Lover

4. See a son! A dawning of a new day
5. Love causes us to see and be seen.
6. *bana*. Bana means "to build or rebuild"
7. sardius, or ruby, the blood of Yeshua
12. the rising sun, mandrake plant, and the man
13. (A) Yeshua and the sons of God, (B) new day, hope, Reubenite (C) breaker anointing
14. The mandrake speaks of Reuben's passionate love, both as his strength and his weakness, giving.
15. giver
19. gifts of mercy, giving, and the gift of helps
21. sight, purity, sight, dominion
28. divine, old Adam

# Chapter 3

## Simeon: The Zealous Hearer

1. The Sh'ma is the declaration the Jewish people recite to affirm their identity, calling, and most of all, their marriage vow to the God of Israel; translated from Hebrew it is taken from Deuteronomy 6:4–5.
2. Mark 12:28–31
4. hearing, know, obey
5. hearing, God has heard
8. very fiery, independent, and strong-willed
14. topaz, chrysolite
15. The yellow topaz represents the glory, wisdom, and is known for hardness; he must rely on the Holy Spirit to deal with this nature and soften him/
19. the sword, earthen pitcher, city gates
20. revival

# Chapter 4

## Levi: The Priestly Bride

4. *"Now this time will my husband be joined unto me"*

7. cohen, draw near

9. To embody and impart the message of being housed with His glory.

10. heavy weight of God's glory, being His very nature

11. purity, circumcised, purified

12. carbuncle or garnet

16. The garnet's origin comes from the Latin word: *granatum*, as in *pomum granatum* ("pomegranate," literally "apple having many seeds");[i] the garnet is similar in color to the pulp of the fruit; the high priest's robe had pomegranates sewn onto it; first fruits company, separation, consecration.

18. 1) He called them to be set apart in order to minister to Him; 2) Levites are intercessors. Their function was to intercede for all the tribes, especially during times of war. They were not to engage in battle naturally, but supernaturally through prayer; 3) Abba knew of Levi's impetuous tendency to defend a righteous cause. In His infinite wisdom, He knew if they engaged in a physical battle, they would be detoured from their spiritual responsibilities and ultimately lose sight of their call. Abba must be Levi's defense; they cannot have any other; 4) Abba was their inheritance.

20. Way, Truth, Life

21. Yeshua

25. bronze mirrors

26. unity in the Body, oracles and revelation Levite called to teach

27. 12

28. Asher, revelatory gift of teaching

31. intercession, worship

32. The lampstand, altar of incense, and the table of shewbread.

33. secret ingredient within the incense, keeping the one thing the one thing, Psalm 27:4

35. Levites, glory

41. ministering to the Lord, intimacy, his sons

54. Houses of prayer, worship, restoring intimacy and holiness

# Chapter 5
## Judah: The Government of Praise

1. praise
2. relationship
3. rule
4. praise
5. Throne-room
6. True praise is a great exhortation, a lifting of another (or something) in esteem, ascribing honor, worth, a recognition of majestic lordship.
7. humility and sincere love
8. magnification
11. emerald
12. emerald green
13. We see that He is our cornerstone, that perfect emerald.
14. green
15. It can also be seen as a symbol of healing (trees of healing for nations) and abundance (in wealth, favor).
17. lion
18. infancy, adolescence, adulthood
21. immaturity
22. leadership, lifetime
23. Seeking the nourishment and counsel of another mature Judah or Levi is needed for a young Judah's development.
24. He is clumsy, making many mistakes in learning the timing and move of the Spirit; he is often whiny, lazy, and prideful; he lacks deep revelation although he shows immediate signs of a powerful prophetic nature and ability; he can be loud, brash, offensive, and even annoying to some.
25. pruning
28. the presence of God, the prophetic, worship
29. The term "wage war" in Hebrew (*tsaba*) means: to do military service, to do a sacred service, and to wait upon the Lord.
30. Judahs must learn to quiet their spirit and allow the Spirit to teach them lessons of servanthood and brokenness.
35. their own Kingdom(s)
36. leaders in the areas of worship, the prophetic, administration, and warfare
37. Satan
38. neglecting the throneroom worship (a holy aroma) and therefore is prey to Satan
45. passionate worshipers, possess, ear, Bridegroom
48. pride

49. pride
52. government, praise
54. lust for power
61. King David's greatest passion was habitation; because of bloodshed, the Lord did not permit David to build His house, but rather Solomon would build it.
62. Levi
63. the wilderness of Maon

# Chapter 6

## Dan: The Voice of Justice

1. Righteousness, justice
2. When we walk according to the laws and precepts of the Father's heart.
3. A voice of justice for the Body.
4. Danites are freedom fighters, deliverance ministers, counselors, teachers, mighty warriors, and great voices of discernment to the Body of Christ.
5. "to judge, vindicate, and to bring justice"
7. blue sapphire
8. The sapphire has been known both for its connections with Heaven (the throne especially) and God's law.
9. two perfect cubes of sapphire
10. judge
11. mercy, judgment
12. He brought deliverance through judges
13. Yeshua, the embodiment of true justice, knowing the cost or penalty of wrongs owed, obtained freedom for us through laying down His own life.
15. The calling of the tribe of Dan is to see justice restored to God's glorious creation.
17. discernment, surrendered
19. not taming his forked tongue
21. Dan's immaturity like that of Judah's in infancy as a lion's whelp; when immature, Dan, like Judah, can find himself in a miry pit of his own pride's doing; Dan's folly of pride lies with the idol of self and judgmental spirit; this is where the anti-Christ spirit will seek territory within Dan.
22. Dan was trying to portray or be a mere copycat of Judah, the lion; this is an anti-Christ spirit.
23. The spirit of anti-Christ is given a foothold when we give into the deception of idolatry of the heart; idols of the heart deny and oppose the true glory of God, seeking their own glory and throne.

# Answer Key

26. Prior to Joshua's conquest of the land, it belonged to the Amorites; it was known for its idolatry and giants that dwelled therein; so Moses, when he prophesies, is saying that Dan is immature (a lion's whelp) leaping into all forms of idolatry such as that of the Amorites; this is a warning of facade(s) for Dan to avoid, rather than an accusation; in greater essence, this prophecy serves as a call to repentance and deliverance for the tribe of Dan; He is questioning Dan; *Why are you associating yourself in idolatry in a territory where I have not placed you, immaturely going into all forms of bondage that negate your true calling of justice?* Dan neglects his calling and communion when he denies his God-given tools of intimacy: wisdom and justice.

30. The Nazarite vow was one of separation and holiness to God; it was a distinction from idolatry and a call to truth .
33. spiritual sight
35. the number seven represents God's perfection
36. The reason was their tendency toward idolatry; Dan did not bind the spiritual strong man in his spiritual house and was thus overtaken by his enemy.
38. Dan, then seeking his own gain, plundered Micah for his idols and overtook and conquered Laish (Judges 18:27–29); once they obtained it, they set up the graven image in it (Judges 18:30–31); Dan's spiral into obscurity started when they neglected to conquer their enemy completely because of compromise in their own hearts.
41. Oholiab was ordained by God to help build the tabernacle in conjunction with Bezalel, who was from the tribe of Judah. It is a beautiful picture of how co-laboring with others works in the Kingdom; justice (Dan and the administration of God's justice), partnering with Judah, the government with praise, helps to build the habitation of the Lord. God longs to bring restoration to the whole house of Israel; within the tribe of Dan you find those gifted in learning and the arts/

# CHAPTER 7

## NAPHTALI : THE DOE SET FREE!

1. to bring liberty in Christ to the captives
2. Naphtali means "to wrestle;" their name is synonymous with their nature both in their strength and facade(s); to wrestle means "to struggle, contest, to strive with arms extended, as two men, who seize each other by the collar and arms, each endeavoring to throw the other by tripping up his heels and twitching him off his center".

3. Identity and destiny of a company of deliverers who would intercede for and become spiritual midwives to His beloved creation; Satan, seeing the glory of God fashioning within the nature of Naphtali, sought to bring confusion and destruction, even abortion to this mighty company of deliverers.
4. submitting to God, worship first
6. through striving, perfectionism, and control
7. formulas and striving; control (Jezebel)
8. When we tolerate the spirit of control, we open ourselves up to all kinds of idol worship, sickness, mind control, and witchcraft; the Jezebel spirit leads us into acts of immorality against the Lover of our soul, Yeshua; to be free of this spirit, we must come into sincere repentance and let go of our need to control or be controlled.
9. Jezebel (or control)
11. life, calling, glory
14. diamond
15. **Strength:** The sharpness of Naphtali's "diamond" can cut away impure motives, idolatry, fear, or anything that hinders perfect love within himself and his fellow living stones; when tempered with love, Naphtali can be used as an instrument of restoration; the diamond also speaks of the charisma and beauty of Naphtali; the very nature of Naphtali attracts many; they are very friendly and hospitable; **Façade:** The danger Naphtali must be on guard for is not allowing his carnal nature of perfectionism and control to wound his brethren; he must avoid being too harsh and controlling.
18. In response to hearing the Word of the Lord, Naphtali will conceive, deliver, and nurture the family of God; in essence, the calling of Naphtali is apostolic in nature; they build the Kingdom through prophetic intercession and wrestling/warfare; not only will they give birth to the revealing of God's sons and daughters, but they are also called to nurture them into a place of habitation.
19. They build the Kingdom through prophetic intercession and wrestling/warfare
21. The deer is a picture of freedom; liberty to the captives, intimacy, and spiritual birthing.
22. call to liberty
24. through forgiveness and repentance
25. First it speaks of the paternal gifting within Naphtali; their words bring comfort, counsel, and direction to the Body; Naphtali's gift of encouragement, whether it be through counsel or prophecy, speaks of the reproductive nature of God; Naphtali's words reproduce the longing of the Father's heart for His creation; this prophecy also further confirms the apostolic nature of this tribe.
26. counseling and discipleship
27. favor, blessing
29. In the natural Naphtali was given the inheritance of the south, which is the Galilee region of Israel God has called for you to possess; when God calls us to possess our

rightful inheritance, he desires for us to possess all His promises, destiny, and dominion granted to us within that inheritance.

30. Through facades of fear, intimidation, striving and control.
31. a) He can either be intimated/afraid, or (b) He can use the tactic of intimidation/fear to others.
32. intimidation and control
33. When we lead others, our calling first and foremost is to serve out of love, not agendas, formulas, and vain ego trips; as spiritual parents to the Body, you must encourage people to hear the Shepherd for themselves.
36. Barak's reluctance caused him to forego the fullness of dominion and destiny; though he was a mighty and heroic general, he shrank in fear at the time of battle.
39. Tabitha displayed her gifting through a hospitable and a nurturing nature; the tribe of Naphtali possesses the gift of hospitality and caring for the poor and afflicted.

# CHAPTER 8

## GAD: THE HABITATION OF GOD'S FORTUNE

1. Habitation, identities
4. blue topaz
5. This rich, beautiful hue speaks of Heaven and of Gad's call not only to habitation, but also to identify with the temporal nature of this present life; when Gad views Yeshua in the light of Heaven and the eternal promises of Heaven, he not only overcomes the enemy, but is drawn into intimacy with his Beloved.
8. nomadic
9. These three tents speak of the Cross and habitation through the work of the Cross; this is Gad's call: to live in the complete work of the Cross; citizenship of heaven, evangelistic call.
10. When Gad ceases from his wandering and settles in his rightful inheritance of habitation, he discovers the treasure within.
11. Jacob is referring to Gad's tug-of-war within himself.
12. Gad's gift of intimacy: faith
17. It is the revelation of the Father Himself that causes Gad's tents to become enlarged.
18. Gad's identity in warfare and their tactics; Gadites can possess the same boldness and gallantry as the tribe of Judah; God chose Gad to emanate the warlike nature of Judah; David himself took notice of these mighty warriors; the nature of Gad is very impressionable (good or bad); they are chameleons, like Reuben, but motivated to do so for different reasons; the primary reasons for this are Gad's insecurity and his very pliable nature; Gad will seemingly take on characteristics of other tribes; Gad is a wanderer, searching to find himself; he tries

on many hats before coming to rest in his own gifting and calling; Gadites may try many different religions, habits, jobs, or relationships when insecure.

21. It was their relentless spirit that caused him to see them in this light; the scripture also says that they were *as swift as a gazelle*; They are swift to run to the cause of freedom and deliverance of their brethren, much like Naphtali; the tribe of Gad identifies with similar aspects of warfare in Moses' prophecy: (a) He lies down as a lion, (b) he tears the arm, and (c) the crown of the head

22. (a) God is calling Gad to engage in battle from the place of rest in the Lord only; engaging from God's rest affords us not to strive in our own abilities or tactics, but to fight with Gad's heavenly weapons of war: faith and habitation; rest is born out of true habitation; when Gad is at rest, he is abiding in the Kingdom's plan laid out before him, knowing that only in Yeshua is victory assured; faith is also born of rest and habitation; (b) Laziness refers to Gad compromising in Numbers 32:6–9, when they settled on the wrong side of the Jordan.

25. Gad will engage in a complete frontal confrontation and assault on the enemy.

26. The crown of the head symbolizes authority; Gad, when tempered by the Spirit in love and humility, will foresee and expose the hypocrisy and falsehoods within his enemy's authority or dominion.

27. prophetic discernment

28. gluttony or a wantonness spirit, a sedentary or lazy spirit, and lying spirits (divination that leads to grave delusion)

29. Gluttony is a driving spirit that will cause us to hunger after the flesh and not Yeshua.

31. fruits of the Spirit, God's character

33. When Gad allows the idols of gluttony and lazy/sedentary spirits full reign, he then spreads out the welcome mat for lying spirits and divination, which will lead to the grave delusion of his soul and mind.

36. the balm of Gilead

38. faith, evangelistic call, prophet, signs and wonders, insecurities, fear of failure, depression, ran from Jezebel, settled because of fear

39. Elijah demonstrated a sincere and compassionate heart of a revivalist when he cried to the Father, *Answer me, O GOD, that Thou art God, and that Thou has turned back their heart again.*

# Chapter 9
## Asher: The Spring of Joy

1. joy
2. Yeshua, joy
5. Asher, breathes, joy

## Answer Key

6. the joy of the Lord
7. Asher imparts revelation, anointing, rich dainties from the Word of God, revival, and intercession through the spring of joy within him.
8. spring, earth
9. anointing, healing, nourishment, and provision to the Body
10. Eight is the number of completion and new beginnings, and Asher is a sign of this covenant to the house of Israel.
11. joy, completion, love
12. to bring strength, nourishment, and refreshing in turbulent times
15. happy, joy, to be joyful, to rejoice, abundance, jubilation
19. agate
20. Agate is fashioned in the hollows of volcanic rocks; a volcano's lava structurally changes whatever form it touches; this is true of the joy of the Lord; the character and nature of Asher is formed through intense fire of the Holy Spirit; it is the process of the heat and pressure that forms rings or bands of color around the agate stone; with each testing and trial, the Holy Spirit refines the character of Asher to bring forth layer upon layer of the beauty and character of God.
23. rest and delight
27. storehouses, outpouring
32. food, will
33. teaching and intercession
34. Asher's teaching ministry is centered on encouragement, mercy, the work of the Holy Spirit, and revival.
36. It is his passion to see his brethren nourished with rich revelation and joy Rueben will give out of love, and Asher will give out of his need to make others happy.
39. our Father's love for us
43. balance, direction
47. Walking in the anointing means not walking in your own strength, abilities, or ideals; it is the essence of the Spirit-led life.
48. Romans 11 speaks of the Jew and Gentile being one in Christ and its relation to the olive tree; we all have obtained joy by being grafted into the Christ; when we are dependent on the Lord and one another to become the One New Man in Him, we will see tremendous outpouring and anointing;
the Gentile needs the Jew to come into the fullness of his anointing, and the Jew is in the need of the Gentile for the fullness of his anointing.
50. compromise, complacency, apathy, man-pleasing
55. Anna—prophetess and intercessor; as any true Asherite, she heralds that the spring of joy (Yeshua) had come to bring deliverance to His people.
56. The tribe of Asher baked the shewbread for the Temple, providing revelation to the Body.

# Chapter 10

Issachar: The Humble Burden Bearer

3. bowing low
4. human, strive
6. To raise, lift up, bear, carry, wear, take, accept, be lifted up, be raised, to be elevated.
8. We must lay down our Kingdoms, ideals, and agendas and to then lift up, extol, and/or magnify the manifest character of God and His glory within us.
9. In order to carry the weight of His Father's Kingdom, Yeshua bowed low and was clothed in humility.
10. majesty and royalty
12. Within Issachar you will find prophets, seer(s)/dreamers, pastors, and administrators with an apostolic mantle.
13. intimacy
15. Issachar means "wages, for hire, servant, [and] his reward will come".
21. Issachar teaches Judah the importance of humility and bowing low, while Judah serves as a voice of affirmation and praise to uplift Issachar's negative tendencies.
22. *Amethyst*, or *Achlamah* in Hebrew, was known as the "dream stone;" in connection with this word is the Hebrew word for dream, *chalam*, meaning to dream prophetically; also speaks of Issachar's calling as a seer.
24. Leadership wanes and becomes profaned when agendas, vanity, and lack of perspective are dominating us; a true minister must serve from intimacy and communion with God,
25. donkey, beast of burden
27. logical, no nonsense
39. The renown of Yeshua, to be that humble yet majestic burden bearer.
41. Abiding, die, rest
46. Zebulun has the call and heart for missions and traveling abroad; Issachar, on the other hand, is the laborer who works to keep things running on the home front.
47. workhorse, tasks
50. pastoral/administrative, mercy motivated
53. worship, works

# Chapter 11
## Zebulun: The Haven for Souls

2. A haven for souls.
3. Great fishers for the souls of the Kingdom
4. prophets, teachers, and missionaries
7. gift, honor, dowry, dwelling, sacrifice
8. Zebulun derives its name from these Hebrew root words: *zebed* (gift), *yizbeleni* (honor), and *zibhe* (sacrifice).
13. wisdom, intimacy
14. sacrifice
18. Spirit, inheritance
20. aquamarine
23. His nature, counsel, and promises
31. restoration
35. idolatry, repentance, glory
38. The gifts of teaching and prophecy.
39. mercy
43. confront, souls

# Chapter 12
## Manasseh: The Forgiving One

1. forgiveness
3. redemption, blood, ransom, reward

4. The **Mercy Seat** was not a mere part of the Ark of the Covenant; it was always a means of access to the very glory and nature of God, a prerequisite.
5. mercy
6. forgiveness and mercy
7. Manasseh means to "**forgive and forget**"
10. The road to forgiveness is paved with great suffering, hard knocks, the disabling of self-righteousness, rude awakenings of human frailties, and finally, the divine intervention and enabling by the grace of God.
11. transformation glory

14. forgiveness, character
15. the bleeding heart of the Father
16. forgiving and forgetting
17. the black onyx
20. shame, freedom, free
23. treasury of rest
24. Onyx is an extremely sensitive and pliable stone that is often used to make cameos.
27. faithfulness, debt, guilt
29. great suffering
29. It carries connotations of righteousness, integrity, beauty, fruitfulness, royalty, rest, and oasis.
33. mirrors, reflection, judges, destiny
35. Cross, Cross
39. forgiveness
40. A "fruitful bough" stems from the Hebrew word **ben** or **bane,** literally translating "**son, a builder of a family name**".
43. Manasseh must take care not to allow their waters to become embittered with the bile of unforgiveness, self-doubt, and fear; doing so will cut them off from the very life source they so desperately need.
45. Suffering, identifier, Cross
47. Manasseh and Ephraim both are called to leadership, specifically an administrative mantle, which may be expressed in callings such as being a pastor, counselor, advisor, administrator, and apostle.
48. Manasseh is low-key and laid back in manner; Manasseh's character often shrinks from the limelight, while his brother Ephraim craves the foreground; Manasseh tends to lean toward passive leadership.
49. Their mother was a Gentile, so He made it clear they were to be adopted into His family; God revealed Yeshua, the head, the great Shepherd and Cornerstone of Israel, welcoming Manasseh and Ephraim into sonship! To a people (meaning the Gentiles) who had not received mercy, he grafted into his family to receive mercy.
53. Theirs is a calling to push, through intercession, apostolic leadership. discipleship, and selfless servant-motivated administration.

# Chapter 13

## Ephraim: The Fruitful Vine

1. Be consumed with the will of the Father
3. self-life
5. Coming into the fullness speaks of maturity, which in essence is fruitfulness; the fullness is where God is calling us that we might become the mature Church through abiding in Christ.
6. fruitful, double fruit, fruitful in the land of affliction
7. Prior to the birth of Manasseh and Ephraim, Egypt had known seven years of plenty; at the time of their births, the seven-year famine had just begun; the land was in serious deprivation, void, and needing redemption; it was not only in that state physically, but spiritually as well; God in His love and mercy births forgiveness (Manasseh) and fruitfulness (Ephraim) during famine; God was adding and multiplying, while Satan was subtracting and dividing.
8. endless, endless
10. Ephraim is a watchman who sees the Kingdom from Heaven's perspective; if you find yourself amongst this noble tribe, you are moved by the plight of the human soul.
11. selfless servant, must take care not to "lord over another," agendas with selfish motives.
13. intercession and servanthood; Ephraim primarily stands in the gap for the redemptive work of the Cross.
16. grapes, abiding on the vine, ox, ox
17. "to seize to be strong, courageous, repair, help, lay hold of, to strengthen, mighty, prevail, to overpower or overcome"
19. repentance
20. reconciliation, abide, repentance
21. transformation, transformed
24. servanthood, strength, harvest, and sacrifice
25. die to the self-life
35. Reproduction, multiply
37. disconnect, world, Christ
38. their first love
40. When our wills become steeped in licentiousness.
41. Abiding in Christ requires the surrender of the will, meaning the full surrender of self and its desire to do its own pleasure.
42. division

# Chapter 14

## Benjamin: The Beloved

3. Benjaminites possess an instinctual awareness that they are truly treasured and loved by God.
5. Benjamin was the only son born after this wrestling; in essence Benjamin was born into destiny—a breaker anointing.
7. Benyamin, Son of My right hand
8. Dominion; by nature and calling they are appointed by God to come into dominion and bid creation to do the same.
10. *Ben-oni*, which means "son of my sorrow;" Rachel's soul was travailing for the loss of children; there is travail within the heart of our heavenly Father for the tribe of Benjamin; in a beautiful type and shadow of Benjamin's two Hebrew names, we see Yeshua revealed; Yeshua became *benoni*, a man of sorrows; we see this in His journey from the Garden of Gethsemane to Calvary.
11. Satan, deliverers, history, warriors
12. Reuben speaks of the beginning of our walk with Yeshua, beginning with the Cross, the work of salvation; through Benjamin, the Beloved speaks of us at the Marriage Supper of the Lamb, the consummation of the ages!
13. Those red markings are the testament of Messiah's blood; the degree of sonship is written all over Benjamin's stone!
16. very eager or greedy for food, satisfaction, or gratification; a *ravenous appetite*, meaning: "excessively grasping or covetous" or "living on prey"
19. Our hearts; the temperature of our hearts determines the bread we feast upon in our souls; when feasting upon the fear of the Lord, Abba bestows fresh, piping hot bread from the ovens of Heaven; however, if we are foolish, we will become like dogs scraping by for stale breadcrumbs.
21. "soul, self, life, creature, person, appetite, mind, living being, desire, emotion, passion, seat of emotions, passions, and appetites, living being"
22. "devour" and "consume"
29. When a Benjamin comes into his lone wolf stage, he is truly being put through the fire, walking his or her own Golgotha; it is when a Benjamin comes into maturity.
31. Benjamin begins his lone wolf stage with the relinquishment of self, a crisis of belief.
33. The secret hidden life is a life of becoming chaste through much refinement where one finds not only maturity, but the fullness of identity and destiny; it is as a lone wolf that Benjamin really comes into who he or she is as the Bride of Christ.
34. worship and obedience

35. A lone wolf comes into full maturity when they have found their mate and begin a pack (or family) of their own; it is only when you lose yourself through the Cross that you gain the fullness of being in *echad* (unity) with your Bridegroom, Yeshua.
36. *who they belong to* and in full maturity of *who they are*
37. security, childlike faith
39. They live in Kingdom reality, inheriting promises in tenacious childlike faith; they refuse to accept the facade of doubt; a Benjamite's faith is a key to his dominion, for he lives his life as Abba's favorite one; they are secure in the love of God.
42. he is enslaved to the lie of the orphan spirit that he is *Benoni, son of sorrows*
45. The first way poverty comes is through an oppression of the enemy, be it through birth (generational curse), sickness (leaving one unable to work and medical bills), a fallen economy, or greed by another afflicting you; the second way poverty comes is through laziness and/or greed (living beyond your means).
48. The nation of Israel did not hunger and thirst after righteousness; they wanted a man-made system to rule them; Israel wanted to do it their way and not God's way; it was after the flesh, self-centered, not presence-driven like King David.
53. rebellion, welcome mat
54. rebellion, witchcraft, and immaturity
55. Self denies the power and the authority of the Cross; to deny the Cross is to deny intimacy, identity, destiny, and dominion; moreover, indulging in the idol of self, which is sin at its core, is to deny sonship.

# Chapter 15

## The New Jerusalem:

### THE HABITATION OF THE LIVING GOD

2. worship (intimacy)
4. To discover how we might take on His reflection found in the embodiment of habitation.
11. holy habitation
12. As we pursue Him, we find fullness of intimacy, identity, destiny, and dominion lie with us possessing *maon kadosh* with Him.
16. Levites to minister to the Lord grafted into the commonwealth of Israel.
17. gifts, fullness
18. The nature of God is infinite; the gifts and callings of God are thereby useful throughout eternity to know Him and work alongside Him in His Kingdom reign; all these things are pertinent to the New Jerusalem and possessing *maon kadosh* with the Father.

19. fullness of identity, intimacy, gifts, and callings found through the tribes
20. The tribes are like families: cumulatively we are one big, happy family; each one of the tribes is a like an immediate family, within which you and I have vital functions to fulfill; each one is valued and different, yet all are celebrated
23. The millennium is the ultimate appointment, 1000-year reign of Christ and honeymoon with His Bride.
28. inheritance
30. identifier, identity
31. Ezekiel's Temple and gates do not contradict the New Jerusalem mentioned in Revelation 21; rather, they make up a clear blueprint that sets the stage for Revelation 21; Ezekiel's gates are a picture of inheritance within the city whereby the King of glory enters into habitation with His Bride.
32. The "heads" speak of our position within our own gate and within our own tribe.
34. ORPHANS!
35. One big happy family reunion!
36. The Temple is the Father's vision by which His Son, Yeshua, will habitat with His Bride; it is the house both He and Yeshua will govern from.

# BIBLIOGRAPHY

Fowler, Marie. *Living Stones.* Lake Wales, FL: Maon Media, 2017.

Zodhiates, Spiros. *The Hebrew-Greek Key Word Study Bible New American Standard Bible Revised Edition.* Chattanooga, TN: AMG Publishers, ©1984, 1990, 2008.

# RESOURCES

**The author recommends the following resources:**

Author and ministry website: www.allgloriouswithin.com
Find us on Facebook: @Author Marie Fowler
Books by Marie Fowler:

*Living Stones: Your Journey into Habitation with the Living God.*
Discover your true identity in this in-depth study on the twelve tribes of Israel. Marie Fowler has spent over twenty-five years of researching, seeking God and His Word to help others become who they were designed to be and to walk in a greater measure of your destiny.

Do you want to be TRANSFORMED into who God designed you to be and find your truest IDENTITY? Do you have roadblocks keeping you from your destiny? Find your place in God's family in *Living Stones*.

"Marie Fowler has given us a MASTERPIECE!
LIVING STONES is an unfolding of the names of the tribes of Israel and how they apply to each of our lives. You'll be amazed as you identify with her teaching and "find your tribe." Read it, study it, embrace it, and find for yourself the Great Mystery of Christ in you and Christ through you! Be sure to get one for your pastor, they will thank you for it!"
- *Dr. Brian Simmons, The Passion Translation Project*

**GET EQUIPPED!**
*Living Stones* is a powerful tool to **EQUIP** you!

*Living Stones* Study Guide is a powerful tool to **EQUIP** you!
- **AWAKEN** to the Glory of God within you as you receive an intimate knowledge of the Father.
- **OVERCOME** the orphan spirit and receive a belonging mindset.

- Each tribe is a facet of the Father's nature (glory). **DISCOVER** your identity in Christ through the Holy Spirit revealing **WHO YOU ARE** as His priceless Living Stone!
- **DEVELOP** *your gifts and callings according to your unique* **SPIRITUAL DNA. LEARN** how to partner with Heaven to develop your strengths found within your tribe.

**AVAILABLE AT:** www.allgloriouswithincom.wordpress.com

*Romancing The Stone: The Greatest Love Story Ever Told, Volume I*

Be serenaded by your Bridegroom Yeshua (Jesus) in this intimate prophetic collection of love letters penned under the leading of the Holy Spirit. You will be swept off your feet and transformed as Yeshua serenades you, His Living Stone- (the Twelve Tribes of Israel). Feel the ache in His heart for you, and know your true worth, the exquisite beauty you truly possess.

Author Marie Fowler has penned *Romancing the Stone* as only she could. Marie spent over twenty-five years researching the twelve tribes of Israel to reveal the true identity of the sons and daughters of God. Years of intercession, worship, and revelation have birthed this from the Bridegroom's passionate heart for you! This tremendous treasure is a face-to-face encounter with the King of Kings Himself. Return to your first love and become undone as you feel His heart breaking from the facades that have detoured you. Experience much healing as His love song restores you to the Father's original design. Be adorned as the brilliant Bride made ready for her Groom. Hear the melodies of angels, the cloud of witnesses standing by, and Heaven's orchestra waiting for their cue as your Bridegroom stands before you face to face and romances you with the love song of the ages!

## IDENTITY UNIVERSITY

*Identity University* (I.D.-U) is a groundbreaking discipleship school dedicated to raising up sons and daughters of God to build the Father's Kingdom. Our great passion is to champion others by revealing their true identity—the very glory of God they possess. We equip you with tools to develop your identity from a place of intimacy, training you in your unique God-given authority, gifts, and callings, while helping you see the facades that have hindered you possessing your identity and the destiny you are meant to fulfill.

If we are in Christ, we are a new creation. We are made in His image. But what does it mean to be made in His image? Who am I as a new creation? What is my destiny? Desperately seeking on her own journey of identity, author Marie Fowler spent twenty-five years researching the tribes of Israel to answer these questions. Using both her many years of study of the twelve tribes, intercession, prophetic insight into the Hebraic roots of the faith and vulnerable teaching style to launch you into your destiny and find your place in God's family! We seek to launch you into your destiny from a **BELONGING MINDSET**. We are a **Pioneer to Pioneers**—Are you called to something so HUGE that it seems so out-of-the-box and impossible?
Congratulations! It means ONLY GOD CAN BRING IT TO PASS! We want to set you up for success. You really are unstoppable!
It would be our absolute joy and privilege to help launch you into the great adventures Abba has planned for you.

**Register today at**: www.allglorouswithincom.wordpress.com

## About the Author...

Marie Fowler's greatest passion is to spend her life at the feet of her extravagant King. Awakened to love at an early age through what would become a lifetime of transformational encounters, Marie lives and ministers from a place of deep intimacy and identity. Whether it be through small home fellowships, worship communities, or houses of prayer, Marie releases revelation and edification to the Bride about her true identity, calling her to awaken to the glory of God within.

Marie is a passionate lover of Israel, advocate, and intercessor. God began to awaken Marie in her own spiritual journey by revealing His heart for Israel and the Jewish people. Marie is dedicated to the restoration of the whole house of Israel: Jew and Gentile, One in Messiah Yeshua (Jesus). She passionately teaches about the One New Man Movement (Ezekiel 37:1–23 and Ephesians 2:15) and is fully invested in seeing this end-time movement come to a glorious full-term birth! Her heart is to release the One New Man (Jew and Gentile) into their truest identity and thus see God's Holy Habitation built—*Living Stone* upon *Living Stone.*

Marie divides her time between the United States and abroad with her adorable fur baby, BJ. She enjoys loving others through her gifts of hospitality and gourmet cooking. If you'd like to connect with Marie for speaking engagements or vendor product inquires, email us at mariefowlerlivingstones@gmail.com

"Now is your appointment with destiny! Like Esther you have been HIDDEN to be REVEALED. You have come into the Kingdom FOR SUCH A TIME AS THIS."
**SO WHAT ARE YOU WAITING FOR? DESTINY AWAITS!**

AUTHOR MARIE FOWLER